TALES

— *from the* —

DUGOUT

TALES

from the

DUGOUT

1,001 Humorous, Inspirational & Wild Anecdotes from Minor League Baseball

Tim Hagerty

CIDER MILL
PRESS

BOOK
PUBLISHERS

Thank you to Al Arrighi for his research and fact-checking assistance.

CONTENTS

FOREWORD

By Billy Butler

A funny story from my minor league days took place in Casper, Wyoming, in 2004. I had just been drafted by the Kansas City Royals out of high school in Jacksonville, Florida, and the Royals assigned me to their MLB affiliate, the Idaho Falls Chukars.

I was playing third base when I noticed there was a live snake in the grass right in front of me. The umpire spotted the snake, put his hands in the air, and stopped the game.

My teammates and I were in the field, keeping our distance from this Wyoming snake, when the Casper Rockies' general manager came down from the stands with a pillow case. He got the snake into the pillow case, brought it off the field, and the game continued.

The Wyoming snake delay is a funny story that I still tell people. You'll read 1,001 more minor league stories in this book.

Billy Butler played in MLB from 2007–2016 with the Kansas City Royals, Oakland Athletics, and New York Yankees. He played in an MLB All-Star Game, a World Series, and won a Silver Slugger Award.

INTRODUCTION

In 2012, I was sifting through newspaper archives for a baseball research project and stumbled upon an incredible story. On July 28, 1888, a Texas League game in Austin was stopped when a wild bull charged onto the field. The bull rumbled around the dirt, kicking up dust, scattering players, and made fans shriek. The game ended early because of the bull's rampage.

I broadcast and write about baseball for a living, and if I hadn't heard this story before, I knew most fans hadn't either. I spent the next decade combing through articles, baseball guides, books, newspapers, the Hall of Fame's files in Cooperstown, New York, conducting interviews, and tracking the latest minor league madness online to compile the most entertaining stories from minor league baseball's past and present—from the base runner who raced a horse, to the catcher who was struck by lightning, to the pitcher who took the mound barefoot.

I hope you enjoy this book!

Tim Hagerty

A TERMINOLOGY NOTE

Every story in this book is connected to an official professional baseball league, and the levels of those leagues have been categorized differently over the years. Organized minor leagues began in 1877, but it wasn't until around 1890 that leagues were assigned different classifications. Class A was the highest and Class F was the lowest. The letters signified the level of play and the level of protection teams had to keep their players from being acquired by other clubs.

Minor League Baseball's levels were renamed in 1963 and the phrases from that makeover are largely still in place today. Triple-A is the highest level with Double-A, High-A, Single-A, and rookie leagues below it. Also, there are, and always have been, independent minor leagues with paid professional players that are outside Major League Baseball's umbrella.

TEAMS & BALLPARKS

SLIPPERY

West Virginia's Wheeling Standards held a Fourth of July picnic in 1877 and the festivities included a contest to see who could catch a greased pig. The winner got to keep the pig.

PLACES TO BE

The New Bedford Whalers played three games in three different cities on the same day in 1878. They began with an 8 a.m. home game in New Bedford, Massachusetts, traveled to Taunton, Massachusetts, for a noon first pitch, and finished the day with nine innings in Providence, Rhode Island, starting at 4 p.m. The hectic day helped the Whalers make up games that were previously postponed.

HELP WANTED

In 1885, the Toronto Baseball Club placed a classified ad in *The New York Clipper* seeking a manager, pitcher, catcher, and other players. The ad demanded that candidates be "sober, reliable, and good batters."

SUIT UP

The Syracuse Stars' uniforms weren't ready for opening day on May 3, 1885, so the Stars took the field in dress suits instead.

FROZEN FUN

Later that year, the Stars played an indoor exhibition baseball game on skates at Cornell University. One batter was given a home run when he hit a ball through the arena's window.

CUBIC ZIRCONIAS?

The Toledo Avengers didn't have enough money to meet payroll in 1885 so they paid players with jewelry.

HIGH TIDE

In the 1890s, after a Galveston Sandcrabs player launched a home run over the outfield fence of the beach-front Beach Park in Galveston, Texas, and into the water, a wave pushed the ball back and stuffed it under the outfield wall. A Houston Buffaloes outfielder picked up the soggy ball and threw out the jogging runner at home plate. After a lengthy argument, the batter was ruled safe and given a homer.

VOODOO

The California League's San Jose Dukes were in a slump in 1891 and the players believed they were cursed, so they piled up their jerseys and bats and burned them to eliminate a potential hex.

THE SIX COMMANDMENTS

In 1891, the Oklahoma City Pirates published these ballpark rules:

1. No intoxicating beverages allowed on the grounds
2. No profane language allowed
3. Betting strictly forbidden
4. Killing of umpire prohibited
5. Absolutely no prostitution allowed on the grounds
6. Horses and carriages allowed on the grounds free of charge

HOME FIELD ADVANTAGE

Two teams played a best-of-19 playoff series in 1891. Pacific Northwest League champion Portland lost to California League champion San Jose, nine games to ten. All 19 games were played in San Jose.

The 19-gamer wasn't the longest scheduled series we found. In 1896, the Texas Association planned a 30-game championship series between Galveston and Houston. After Houston won five of the first seven games, the series was called early and Houston was declared the winner.

WHERE ARE YOU?

The Buffalo Bisons and Rochester Flour Cities didn't play on July 15, 1892, because both teams waited at their own ballparks, thinking it was a home game.

In a similar miscommunication, San Diego Padres and Texas Rangers minor leaguers were set to play a spring training game on March 15, 2017, but the Padres sent their prospects to the Rangers' facility and the Rangers sent theirs to the Padres' facility.

BRIDGE

In the early 1900s, the Class B New York State League's Troy Trojans placed wooden boards on the ground to cover a river that cut through their outfield.

TAPE MEASURE

The Denison Tigers started the 1896 Texas Association season with a pitcher's mound that was 70 feet from home plate, 9.5 feet farther than it should've been.

In related news, first base was 87 feet from home plate, instead of 90, at the San Diego Padres' new Pacific Coast League ballpark in 1936.

DRESS CODE

The Toledo Mud Hens protested their 12-11 loss to Fort Wayne on April 30, 1899, because the game-winning hit came from a Fort Wayne player who wasn't wearing a uniform.

SLAGGING ROOM ONLY

West End Park in Birmingham, Alabama, was unofficially called "The Slag Pile" in the early 1900s because of quarry workers who watched games from slag heaps behind the fence. (Slag heaps are piles of excess material from industrial sites or mines.)

NO WARNING TRACKS

Ramona Park, the early 1900s Class B Central League stadium in Grand Rapids, Michigan, had a dirt outfield and a grass infield.

Bonneville Park in Salt Lake City hosted minor league games from 1915–1927. For some of those seasons, it had a grass infield and gravel outfield.

SPRING TRAIN-ING

Traveling by train reminded the Wilkes-Barre Barons of their early 1900s home stadium, Artillery Park: the outfield fence there was made of railroad boxcars.

UNDER THE BIG TOP

In the early 1900s, the Class A Louisville Colonels pitched a circus tent over their infield to protect the field from rain.

WORTHLESS?

Residents of Atlanta turned down a free offer to own the Southern Association's Atlanta Firemen in 1901, feeling as if the club had no value. Within 10 years, the franchise was valued at $75,000. These days, some minor league teams are worth tens of millions.

PARK FACTORS

Lowell and Augusta had to move a New England League game to a makeshift park in Gardiner, Maine, on May 25, 1901. The temporary site had a hill in right field, a river running through center field, and a stone wall in left field.

STALKING

After Lowell won a road game in Concord, New Hampshire, on June 30, 1901, Concord fans followed Lowell's players back to the team hotel and threw rocks at them.

RELIGIOUS RELOCATION

The Class D Corsicana Oil Citys had a Texas League home game scheduled for Sunday, June 15, 1902, but it was against the law to play baseball on Sundays in Corsicana. The game moved to a temporary ballpark in Ennis, Texas, with a right field fence only 210 feet from home plate. Left-handed batter Justin Clarke hit eight home runs that day in Corsicana's 51-3 smashing of Texarkana, still a professional baseball record for home runs in a game.

NO DIRECTION HOME

The Minneapolis Millers showed up late to their own ballpark. The Millers had a triple-header vs. Louisville on September 22, 1902, but had to forfeit Game 1 because they didn't arrive on time.

YOUNGEST PLAYER EVER?

The Class B Concord Marines brought only ten players to their New England League game in Lowell, Massachusetts, on June 25, 1904. Their catcher left because of illness in the fourth inning and the second baseman was ejected in the sixth, leaving them with only eight players. They asked nine-year-old George Diggins, the son of the sick catcher, to stand in right field. Little George didn't have any fielding chances and he struck out in his only at bat.

A BALLPARK IN TWO STATES

The Texarkana Casketmakers' stadium straddled the Arkansas-Texas state line in 1902. Home plate, first base, and third base were in Arkansas, while second base and the outfield were in Texas.

FORECLOSURES

In 1906, Americans could buy newspapers for a penny and toothpaste for a quarter. They could also buy a professional baseball team for $25. The Class B Norwich Reds were in financial turmoil and ownership of the team was auctioned at a sheriff's sale. D. J. Morrissey paid $25 and became the newest Connecticut State League owner.

In 1955, the Triple-A Richmond Virginians couldn't pay their bills so the franchise was sold for $20,000 at an IRS auction at the ballpark.

TAKING A DIVE

The Class C San Antonio Bronchos walked off the field to protest a call in Game 1 of a doubleheader in Austin, Texas, on July 23, 1907. The team refused to play and the umpire ruled it a forfeit.

The Bronchos intensified their protest by intentionally losing Game 2. They used infielders as pitchers, let fly balls drop, allowed a Texas League-record 23 stolen bases, and lost 44-0.

HOUSE OF ILL REPUTE

The 44-0 tanking wasn't the last time the Bronchos behaved questionably. They held a team party at a brothel to celebrate their 1908 Texas League championship.

SLUGGER-FOR-STADIUM SWAP

Hall of Famer Tris Speaker was traded for a ballpark. The Boston Red Sox sent Speaker to the Class A Little Rock Travelers in 1908, and in exchange, Boston got to use Little Rock's park for spring training. Speaker hit .350 in 127 Travelers games before the Red Sox reacquired him.

DREADFUL

The awful Oakland Commuters finished with a 4-73 record in 1908, the pitiful Paducah Indians lost 27 straight games in 1922, and, in 1951, the gruesome Granite Falls Graniteers lost 26 games in row, won one game, then lost another 33 consecutive games to close the season.

ROADSIDE REPAIR

The Class D Kentucky-Illinois-Tennessee League's Jackson Generals lost 36 straight games in 1954, including one forfeit when they didn't show up because of bus trouble.

38 SPECIAL

The Class C Muskogee Mets surpassed Jackson's futility with a 38-game losing streak in 1923, setting the professional baseball record for most consecutive losses. Amazingly, they weren't the worst team in the Southwestern League that year; the Independence Producers produced only 49 wins, while the M-Mets won 57.

A TRANCE

In 1911, an unnamed minor leaguer claimed he wasn't paid by his team and was hypnotized into believing that he was paid.

WHAT A FINISH!

On September 10, 1910, the Fayetteville Highlanders clinched the Class D Eastern Carolina League championship by turning a triple play to end a 2-1 win over Rocky Mount.

GAME BALL

Kansas City and Columbus played a whole game with the same baseball on April 11, 1912. These days, minor league teams use more than 150 balls a game.

IN DEBT

In 1912, the Class D Western Canada League's Bassano Boosters dismantled their ballpark and sold the lumber to pay off player salaries that were past due.

SPIKING THE SERIES

The Johnson City Soldiers won the 1913 Class D Appalachian League championship via forfeit. The team was furious after a Knoxville Reds runner slid into, kicked, and injured their infielder. Johnson City threatened retaliation and the scared Reds refused to finish the series.

MOTOCROSS

The Class D Valdosta Millionaires' field was surrounded by a dirt motorcycle racing track in Valdosta, Georgia, from 1913–1916.

BLURRED LINES

The San Francisco Seals moved from old Recreation Park to new Ewing Field in 1914 and their new stadium was the talk of the town. Then the season started and the excitement, and the pop-flies, disappeared. Ewing Field was built in a spot with nightly dense fog and fly balls were regularly lost in the murky weather. The Seals returned to their old ballpark, despite spending $100,000 on the new one, because of the constant fog.

RENTED MULE

The Class A New Orleans Pelicans moved their stadium a few blocks down the street in 1914 and used a group of mules to drag the wooden grandstands to the new location.

BALLPARK ON WHEELS

In 1915, Venice Tigers owner Peter Maier moved his team and brought the stadium with him, without the help of mules. The Tigers' ballpark was taken apart in Venice, California, loaded onto trucks, and transported 20 miles down the road to Vernon, California. The stadium was rebuilt identically in the new spot.

Maier picked Venice and Vernon because they were the only two towns in the county where liquor could be sold.

IF YOU BUILD IT . . .

The Class D Chambersburg Maroons played on a converted cornfield in 1915. The team couldn't charge admission because fans could walk through the cornstalks and see the game.

FIELD OF DREAMS

The Double-A Portland Sea Dogs create a similar scene each year on Fan Appreciation Day when their players walk through temporary cornfields in the outfield while wearing 1920s Portland Eskimos throwback uniforms.

LONG DAY

The Durham Bulls and Raleigh Capitals played 35 innings spread between two games and two ballparks on July 5, 1915. First, they competed for 14 innings in Raleigh, North Carolina, then traveled 25 miles to Durham, North Carolina, and endured a 21-inning game there.

BARNYARD

The Class D Frederick Hustlers took the phrase "farm system" literally. Their ballpark had barns in left field from 1915–1917.

A TALE OF TWO CITIES

Vancouver moved to Vancouver in 1918. When British Columbia's Vancouver Beavers refused to make a road trip, the Class B Pacific Coast International League banished them. The franchise moved 300 miles south to Vancouver, Washington, and they didn't even have to change their uniforms.

SMUGGLING

The Class A Chattanooga Lookouts bought two players and a case of whiskey from the Class B Peoria Tractors for $2,000 in 1920. Tractors management had to secretly deliver the whiskey because it was during prohibition.

OBSTACLES

In 1921, there were telephone poles and a schoolhouse on the field and in play at the home park of the Class D Northern Utah League team in Smithfield.

COPY AND PASTE

The Class A Fort Worth Panthers used the exact same lineup for all 148 games in 1921 and won the Texas League championship that year.

VARSITY

The Double-A Tulsa Drillers had to play at a high school field in 1977 after a grandstand collapsed at Driller Park during a preseason exhibition between the Houston Astros and Texas Rangers.

CAR TROUBLE

Blue Ridge Leaguers ran and ran some more on trips to Gettysburg, Pennsylvania. Nixon Field, the Class D Gettysburg Patriots' home, didn't have an outfield fence in 1915. Deep outfield hits rolled endlessly.

Nixon Field didn't have a parking lot either, so cars parked in the outfield. Fielders crawled under automobiles to retrieve batted balls because the ground rules said under-the-engine baseballs were in play.

MUSCLE FOR MUSSELS

The Class A Dallas Submarines traded pitcher Joe Martina to New Orleans for two barrels of oysters in 1921.

ARE YOU LOST?

The Class D Eastern Shore League's Cambridge Canners signed 18-year-old George Selkirk in 1927. When Selkirk arrived, he accidentally entered the clubhouse of the opposing team, the Crisfield Crabbers, who were also expecting a new player.

Selkirk played that day for Crisfield before anyone realized he was supposed to be playing for Cambridge. The confusion was resolved after the game and he switched teams.

FIRST IN FLIGHT

The Hollywood Stars boarded a plane and flew from Seattle, Washington, to Portland, Oregon, during a road trip in 1928, becoming what is believed to be the first professional baseball team to travel by airplane.

Many players had a fear of flying during this era. In 1929, baseball executives voted down a proposal to place a Class B team in Havana, Cuba, because it would've required players to fly there throughout the season.

CHANGING COLORS

The American Association's Louisville Colonels and Milwaukee Brewers played a game with yellow baseballs on August 28, 1928. They thought yellow balls would be easier to see and harder to stain with dirt.

ONE-NIGHT STAND

Maud, Oklahoma, swung and missed at its only chance to get professional baseball. The Class C Muskogee Chiefs relocated there on August 22, 1929, hoping for better profits, but after one sparsely attended game, management decided to play the rest of the season on the road. Maud never got another minor league team.

SLEEPING ON THE JOB

Dozens of Class C players slept near cannibals in the 1930s. The East Texas League's Longview Cannibals slept at their ballpark after home games. They put ice beneath their sheets to keep cool.

HIGH BEAMS

Some minor league teams hosted night games in the 1930s, but the Class C Johnstown Johnnies couldn't afford ballpark lights, so they illuminated their field by stringing together car headlights and attaching them to telephone poles.

SUPER WINGS

The Chattanooga Lookouts organized national pigeon races in the 1930s. Birds and their owners came to Chattanooga, Tennessee's Engel Stadium from 25 cities and 10 states. The competing birds flew hundreds of miles and were timed.

BIRDS OF A FEATHER

Carrier pigeons flew from the Class C Ventura Braves' ballpark to radio station KVEN to deliver live updates of the Braves' exhibition game against Fresno on April 11, 1952. The station's sportscasters usually announced play-by-play based on Western Union telegraph updates, but there was a telegraph operators strike, so they got their information from the birds.

THE TREE IS FIRST BASE

The Pacific Coast League's Seattle Indians played on an improvised field in a city park in 1932 after their stadium burned down.

GO TO HULL

The Canadian-American League's Ottawa Braves avoided baseball-banning blue laws in the 1930s by moving all Sunday home games from Ottawa, Ontario, to Hull, Quebec.

HONOR THE SABBATH

Sunday baseball bans were no joke. The entire Class B Schenectady Frog Alleys roster was arrested on May 25, 1903, when they were caught playing on a Sunday.

BE QUIET

It was also against the law to play ball on Sundays in Jersey City, New Jersey, in 1909, so the Jersey City Skeeters hosted a home exhibition secretly on April 18 that year. They distributed cards telling fans that cheering wasn't allowed.

THEY WEREN'T BLUFF-ING

The Class C Dixie League had to reshuffle its schedule late in the 1933 season because every Pine Bluff Judges player quit with a week left.

WE'RE BACK!

The Watertown Bucks found that the grass isn't always greener. The Bucks relocated 90 miles away to become the Massena Grays on June 24, 1936, but moved back to Watertown, New York, after only two weeks of poorly attended cold-weather games in Massena, New York.

SURVEYOR ERROR

Tacoma, Washington's ballpark was laid out incorrectly for 30 years. The foul lines were accidentally drawn at an 84.5-degree angle instead of 90, making the outfield 15 feet too small. The mistake was fixed in 1937, but not before thousands of foul balls landed that should've been called fair.

TAXI SQUAD

The Class D Eastern Shore League's Salisbury Indians racked up expensive cab fares in 1937. The team bus broke early in the season, so they hired a taxi company to transport players to all remaining road games.

CARPOOL

The Class B Asheville Tourists toured the Piedmont League in style in 1938. The Tourists were owned by a luxury car dealer, so they traveled to away games in fancy seven-seater Packards.

WATCHDOG

In 1939, the Minneapolis Millers kept an angry Dalmatian in the right field corner to growl at visiting outfielders.

RAMPING UP

In the late 1930s, the Class C Akron Yankees' ballpark had a left field fence that slanted back. Outfielders sometimes ran up the fence trying to make catches.

STEAK BREAK?

The Class D Kentucky-Illinois-Tennessee League's Fulton Eagles were wearing down in the fifteenth inning on July 8, 1938, so their manager, Ray Clonts, requested a 15-minute break so his players could eat some steak. The umpire said no.

RUBBISH

Ruppert Stadium, home of the International League's Newark Bears in the 1940s, was next to a city dump and sometimes games were delayed by thick smoke from burning garbage.

STREET CLOTHES

The Class D Wausau Timberjacks changed into their uniforms in the hotel before their road game in Superior, Wisconsin, on June 19, 1940. As the game unfolded, the hotel burned down, and the players' personal clothes were lost in the fire. With nothing to change into, the team wandered around town in full uniform after the game, looking for a new place to stay.

SHIVERING SPRING TRAINING

In the early 1940s, the Class C Quebec Athletics held spring training near the National Baseball Hall of Fame in Cooperstown, New York. While it was chilly and snowy in upstate New York, it was still warmer than Quebec.

BORROWED CLOTHES

The Eastern League's Springfield Nationals forgot to bring jerseys to a 1941 road series against the Wilkes-Barre Barons, so they borrowed jerseys from the Barons and turned them inside out during games.

EXTREME MAKEOVER, BALLPARK EDITION

The Class C Amsterdam Rugmakers' stadium burned down just eight days before a hyped exhibition against the New York Yankees, which was scheduled for July 20, 1942. The Yankees didn't believe the game could be played, but groups of Amsterdammers shocked everyone by rebuilding Mohawk Mills Park in eight days. The Yankees came to town and the game happened in front of 4,032 fans.

MISSED BASE

A blackout in Lancaster, Pennsylvania, shut off the lights during a Class B Interstate League Championship Series game on September 29, 1943. A fan snuck onto the field, stole second base, and ran away with it into the darkness. The game was delayed 20 minutes as the umpire looked for a new base.

BATTLEFIELD

The Pacific Coast League's Oakland Oaks postponed two games in the mid-1940s after their playing surface was destroyed by the United States Cavalry, who used the field for World War II training exercises.

HOMELESS ORPHANS

In August 1947, the Lowell Orphans got evicted from their ballpark in Massachusetts after losing 20 consecutive games and drawing only 85 fans to a doubleheader. They had to finish the season on the road.

IRONY

The Sacramento Solons' ballpark burned down on July 11, 1948, forcing the team to play all remaining games on the road. The Solons didn't have to buy new uniforms because their road jerseys and pants were at the cleaners at the time of the fire.

GRAB A MAP

Five different cities named Greenville hosted minor league baseball teams in 1948: Greenville, Alabama; Greenville, Mississippi; Greenville, North Carolina; Greenville, South Carolina; and Greenville, Texas.

BAD BLUEPRINTS

When the Class B Newport News Dodgers' press box was knocked down in a hurricane in the 1940s, the construction crew rebuilt it facing the wrong direction. The windows faced the parking lot and not the field.

SHORT SHORTS

The Class C Abilene Blue Sox wore shorts for two games in August 1950. The Blue Sox ditched the shorts because the players were covered in mosquito bites after both games.

DEEP CENTER

In the late 1940s and early 1950s, the Class D Pennington Gap Miners played in a ballpark in Virginia where the center field fence was 1,400 feet from home plate. These days, the deepest outfield fence at a minor league park is 428 feet from home in Albuquerque, New Mexico.

IMPOUND LOT

The Class C Sunset League's Tijuana Colts had their team bus impounded twice during the 1949 season because of unpaid hotel bills.

WHAT A DRAG

In 1950, the Pacific Coast League's Hollywood Stars asked their grounds crew to drag the infield dirt once a game, hoping a break in the action would spur fans to leave their seats and buy concessions. Many say this started the baseball tradition of dragging the infield during games.

EN VOGUE

The Stars brought Hollywood style to the Pacific Coast League. The team's uniforms in the 1950s included pinstriped shorts, knee socks, and silk shirts with collars.

A BALL IN THE HAND
BEATS TWO IN THE BUSH

The Class B Tri-State League's Asheville Tourists used bushes to cheat in the 1950s. The team strategically hid baseballs in the outfield shrubs, then would yank one out during a game, pretending the planted ball was the live ball. League officials busted them one night after two outfielders threw baseballs in simultaneously.

PEANUT PROHIBITION

The San Francisco Seals banned peanuts in 1950. Seals owner Paul Fagan was losing money from paying employees to clean up peanut shells and he controversially stated "the goober has to go." Fans flooded the ballpark phone lines and some planned to bring in their own peanuts and drop shells in the aisles. The peanut protests worked—by opening day, peanuts were back at Seals Stadium.

OFF-DUTY

In the 1950s, the Class A Eastern League's Schenectady Blue Jays hired a police officer to patrol the exterior of their ballpark on a motorcycle and scoop up foul balls before fans could. They also hung netting around the stadium to capture foul balls and save money.

OPEN-AIR CLUBHOUSE

A tornado in Elizabethton, Tennessee, ripped the roof off Cherokee Park's visiting clubhouse in 1951, so Appalachian League teams had to change clothes in a locker room without a ceiling. There were loose nails and poison ivy on the wrecked walls.

THE CLINK

In 1956, the Class B Abilene Blue Sox arrived for a road series in Corpus Christi, Texas, and every hotel room in town was taken. Manager Al Evans made some calls and booked an overnight stay in the county jail. Players shared wooden slabs inside jail cells.

ZIM

Legendary baseball figure Don Zimmer got married on the field at Dunn Field in Elmira, New York, on August 16, 1951. Zimmer played for the Class A Elmira Pioneers later that night and got three hits.

PLOWING THROUGH THE OPPOSITION

The Class B Miami Beach Flamingos gave manager Pepper Martin a bulldozer as a reward for his winning season in 1954. Martin used it on his off-season ranch in Oklahoma.

SPLENDID SPLINTERS

Oaks Park in Oakland, California, was so old in the 1950s that line drives off the outfield wall sent pieces of wood fluttering to the ground.

INFIGHTING

Lynchburg Senators manager Chick Payne was ejected from a game in Lynchburg, Virginia, in 1959 and the team didn't have any other coaches to take over. Players tried to govern themselves but a disagreement over playing time turned into a melee, with punches thrown. The game was delayed as police broke up the dugout altercation. Cops sat in the dugout for the remaining innings.

CAMPFIRE

The Triple-A Havana Sugar Kings traveled from Cuba to Minnesota for a playoff series in September 1959. Havana players were so cold that they stacked paper in a trash can, put the trash can in the middle of the dugout, and lit the paper on fire to keep warm.

TERMITE SEASON

The Triple-A Hawaii Islanders were bugged by their stadium's uninviting nickname. Honolulu Stadium was unofficially called "Termite Palace" because the wooden stadium was infested with termites. When the Islanders moved to a new stadium in 1975, insect researchers used the old park for a termite experiment.

SIZZLING SCOREBOARD

A scoreboard fire made a long game even longer on April 29, 1960. Double-A San Antonio was batting in the bottom of the twenty-third inning against Rio Grande Valley when the scoreboard caught fire. Ballpark employees extinguished the flames and the marathon game continued with a smoke-filled outfield.

SHOPPING SPREE

The Class A Yakima Braves lost their uniforms and equipment in a bus fire on May 3, 1963. Their next game, in Salem, Oregon, was delayed 45 minutes as Braves players roamed a local sporting goods store to buy new gear.

BORDERLINE HOMERS

Mexican Rookie League home runs needed passports in 1968. The Mexico-based Agua Prieta Charros played in a ballpark along the Arizona border. Long balls past the left field fence flew from Mexico into the United States.

SITE OF SEVEN SUPER BOWLS

The Triple-A New Orleans Pelicans played home games at the Louisiana Superdome in 1977. More than 215,000 fans flocked to see the Pelicans that year, some of whom went just to see the massive dome's baseball configuration. The Pelicans left the Superdome after one season because rent costs were too high.

HONK FOR HOMERS

There was drive-in baseball in New Mexico at Albuquerque Sports Stadium from 1969–2000. A plateau above the outfield wall gave parked cars an elevated view and fans beeped their car horns after Albuquerque home runs.

MISSED BY A DECADE

The Albuquerque Dodgers accidentally celebrated a 110th anniversary. The Dodgers wore old-fashioned uniforms and mustaches on June 12, 1969, to honor a baseball centennial, but the stitching on the jerseys said "1859" instead of "1869."

A CRYING SHAME

Albuquerque Sports Stadium filled with tear gas on June 13, 1971, interrupting that night's game twice. The tear gas drifted from a riot four blocks away.

DON'T DIVE

Left field was made of cement for a minor league game in 1969. Portland, Oregon's Civic Stadium was in the process of becoming the first Triple-A park to use Astroturf, but the installation wasn't completed in time. The new turf didn't cover left field, where the grounds crew painted the concrete green. The remaining Astroturf was laid down before the next game.

STOLEN GAME

July 19, 1969, was a sunny night in western New York, yet the Triple-A Buffalo Bisons game was postponed because of a robbery the night before. A gang broke into the Bisons clubhouse, threatened players with knives, and stole their money. The team felt unsafe and refused to play until stadium security was upgraded. The Bisons' postponement announcement fibbed and cited "threatening weather" as the reason.

STEALING SIGNS

The Eugene Emeralds' scoreboard operator got caught using binoculars to watch Tacoma's catchers' signals during the 1969 Triple-A Pacific Coast League Championship Series. The scoreboard employee was positioned in center field and relayed what he saw to Eugene's batters using hand gestures. The umpire caught him and confiscated the binoculars.

EXTRA INNINGS

Two Double-A Eastern League teams accidentally played an extra game in 1969. Five early-season Elmira Pioneers-Waterbury Indians games were rained out that year and all of those postponements had to be made up through doubleheaders later in the summer. Neither team, nor the league office, noticed that the two clubs ended up playing each other 29 times, instead of the scheduled 28. The extra game counted and both teams finished with 141 games played instead of 140.

NEXT-DOOR NEIGHBORS

The Double-A Bristol Red Sox crossed paths with their opponents after each half inning during 1970s home games. The dugouts were side-by-side behind third base at Muzzy Field in Bristol, Connecticut. The BriSox even had a fight with the Quebec Carnavals in front of the dugouts in 1974.

TILT

In the 1970s, scouts got slanted opinions of infielders at the same ballpark in Bristol, Connecticut. The infield leaned at an incline, helping some players run downhill and hurting others running uphill.

I SWEAR

The Portland Mavericks weren't friendly visitors. The 1970s independent team had a road trip tradition of rolling down their bus windows and shouting obscenities at people on the sidewalk.

SPORTS PSYCHOLOGY

The Single-A Midwest League's Waterloo Royals were mired in a losing streak in the summer of 1971 so six players went to a hypnotist to focus their minds on the next game. The hypnosis didn't work; Waterloo lost 10–2 the next night.

A LOCKOUT

The Double-A Texas League's Midland Cubs wanted to take batting practice on April 19, 1972, the day their new stadium opened, but they couldn't because the baseballs were locked in a shed and nobody had the key.

THE SHORTEST PORCH

Hughes Stadium, the mid-1970s home of the Triple-A Sacramento Solons, was a converted football stadium and its left field wall was only 233 feet from home plate. A 40-foot screen didn't stop home run barrages there–250 of Sacramento's 305 homers in 1974 came in home games.

23 FEET TALLER THAN THE GREEN MONSTER

Maybe Sacramento should've hired the Toledo Mud Hens' architects. Toledo's ballpark from 1897–1909 had a 60-foot-tall brick left field wall with towers at the top that made it resemble a medieval castle.

LONGEST GAME IN HISTORY

The Triple-A Pawtucket Red Sox' 33-inning win over the Rochester Red Wings in 1981 took eight hours and 25 minutes, spread out over two days, to finish. Future Hall of Famer Cal Ripken Jr. came to bat 15 times for Rochester. Fellow future Hall of Famer Wade Boggs played in the record-setting game for Pawtucket.

BE ALERT

The Single-A Beloit Brewers forgot to hang their screen behind home plate in 1982 in Beloit, Wisconsin. After a batter fouled a pitch straight back into the stands on opening night, the team installed netting.

GOT A MATCH?

The Bakersfield Mariners and Visalia Oaks were battling late into the night during a 1982 Single-A California League doubleheader when the sprinklers came on and flooded the field. Once the sprinklers were shut off, Bakersfield's staff lit the field on fire to dry up the puddles. The plan worked, the game resumed, and Bakersfield's grass stayed yellow for the rest of the season.

ZONING LAWS

Relentless rain swamped Double-A El Paso's outfield grass in 1984, and instead of cancelling a few games, the team roped off the saturated block of grass and played. Temporary ground rules stated that any ball hit into the roped off section was an automatic single.

105 FEET LONG!

The Double-A El Paso Diablos handed out spoons and had kids share what the team called "The World's Largest Banana Split" on April 21, 1974. It contained 170 bananas, 15 gallons of ice cream, 12 gallons of strawberries, and 15 pounds of whipped cream.

BOY BAND

The Double-A Texas League's Midland Angels showed they could carry a tune on August 24, 1987. The national anthem singer didn't show up before their road game in El Paso, Texas, and Plan B fell through when the music operator couldn't play a recording, so Midland's players lined up in front of the dugout and sang the anthem together. The fans cheered enthusiastically.

BEAN COUNTING

Billy Bean and Billy Beane both played for the 1988 Triple-A Toledo Mud Hens. They even shared the same outfield sometimes.

ANOTHER NAME GAME

The 2005 Triple-A Nashville Sounds had two players named Corey Hart and their first and last names were spelled the same. One Corey Hart pinch-hit for the other on June 26 of that year.

LET'S PLAY THREE

Colorado Springs and Calgary played each other three times on August 2, 1988. The purpose of the Triple-A triple-header was to finish a suspended game, make up a postponed game, and play their regularly scheduled game.

OR LET'S NOT

On May 3, 2016, the High-A Carolina League's Potomac Nationals and Lynchburg Hillcats announced they would play a triple-header to make up rained-out games. One day later, after input from their major league affiliates, the teams announced they'd play a standard doubleheader and make up the third game on a different day.

TARP TAMPERING

A group of Single-A Wausau Timbers players didn't want to play a doubleheader on August 13, 1990, in South Bend, Indiana, so they broke into the ballpark on the rainy night before and yanked the tarp off the field. The uncovered field got drenched but South Bend's grounds crew got the last laugh when they dried the field and watched the entire doubleheader with a smile.

THEY GOT GAME

Charlotte Hornets NBA players Muggsy Bogues and Dell Curry played for the Single-A Gastonia Rangers against the Spartanburg Phillies on June 21, 1991. Bogues played second base and went 0 for 2 with two strikeouts while Curry pitched three innings and struck out four batters. Hornets owner George Shinn also owned the Rangers and arranged their one-game stint.

A DOZEN GAMES

The Double-A Shreveport Captains had to play six consecutive doubleheaders in 1992 because of repeated rainouts.

A RECORD RECORD

The Toronto Blue Jays won the World Series in 1992. That same year, the Blue Jays' Dominican Summer League team had one of the best records in professional baseball history. The "D-Jays" went 68-2, won 37 consecutive games to start the season, and finished 36.5 games ahead of the second place squad.

While Toronto received World Series rings, the Dominican Summer Leaguers left empty-handed. They lost in the first round of the play-offs.

GOOD CATCH

The independent Pacific Suns traded pitcher Ken Krahenbuhl to the Greenville Bluesmen for 10 pounds of Mississippi catfish in 1998. Krahenbuhl threw a perfect game in his first start with the Bluesmen.

FLY-BY-NIGHT

The Waterloo Diamonds couldn't secure a stadium lease in 1994 and the team was evicted by the City of Waterloo two weeks before opening day. The Single-A squad migrated to Springfield, Illinois, where players wore hand-me-down San Diego Padres jerseys in April because the new Springfield uniforms weren't ready.

VIOLENCE NEVER WINS

Durham and Winston-Salem picked the worst time to have a benches-clearing brawl. The High-A Bulls and Warthogs fought on the field for more than 20 minutes on May 22, 1995, which was "Strike Out Domestic Violence Night" at Durham's ballpark.

STONES

Medicine Hat, Alberta, Canada, hosted minor league baseball from 1997–2002. The ballpark was in the same athletic complex as the city's curling center.

PRIDEFUL

The Nashua Pride had Curtis Pride on their roster in 1999 and from 2003–2004. The Pride were an independent Atlantic League team based in New Hampshire.

ANOTHER NAME ON THE FRONT AND BACK OF THE JERSEY

Austin Nola played for the Triple-A New Orleans Zephyrs in 2015, a club whose home jerseys read "NOLA" on the front, an abbreviation for New Orleans, Louisiana.

OFFICE DRAMA

In an unusual overlap of player development contracts, Single-A Midwest League rivals Clinton and Dayton were both Cincinnati Reds' affiliates in 2000. They even had a benches-clearing fight that year.

BOARDWALK BASEBALL

The independent Atlantic City Surf public address announcer read a nightly message in the early 2000s asking fans not to feed the seagulls.

STUNG

The Triple-A Salt Lake Buzz changed their name to Stingers in 2001 after a years-long court battle with Georgia Tech University, who filed a copyright lawsuit because their school's mascot is named Buzz.

EXTRA ROOMS

The independent Fort Worth Cats' ballpark had four dugouts. The Cats renovated LaGrave Field in 2001 and added new dugouts but they kept the old ones too.

DRY PARTY

The Provo Angels were the only team in baseball that preferred clinching a championship on the road. The rookie league club shared their stadium with Brigham Young University's baseball team and the ballpark was on BYU's campus, where alcohol is banned. Provo swept Billings to win the 2004 Pioneer League championship and players sprayed soda, not champagne, in their clubhouse celebration.

FAIR POINT

The Jacksonville Suns tried to adjust baseball's dictionary in 2007. The Double-A team renamed their foul poles "fair poles" and introduced them that way on the stadium speakers and game broadcasts before every game. Suns management felt foul poles should be called "fair poles" since the poles are in fair territory.

HOMETOWN HERO

Hank Aaron Stadium in Mobile, Alabama, hosted Double-A Southern League games from 1997–2019. In 2008, Aaron's childhood home was moved from a Mobile neighborhood to the ballpark and converted into a museum displaying artifacts from his legendary career.

WE QUIT

The Triple-A Tucson Sidewinders forfeited one game of their season-ending doubleheader in 2008 because they didn't have enough pitchers.

UNDERDOGS

The High-A Winston-Salem Dash beat their parent club, the Chicago White Sox, 3-0 in a 2011 exhibition game in Winston-Salem, North Carolina. Minor league teams have defeated their MLB affiliates at least 10 times since 1993, with the most lopsided example being the Toledo Mud Hens' 14-1 win over the Detroit Tigers in 1996.

HOSED

Fans in Lancaster, California, were confused to hear the High-A Lancaster JetHawks game was postponed because of wet field conditions on August 30, 2011, because it hadn't rained. It was a man-made rainout; the grounds crew over-watered the field before the game and the puddles were considered a safety hazard for the players.

BALLPARK BABY

Pregnant Bradenton Marauders fan Latisha Kirk went into labor while at the team's preseason open house at McKechnie Field on February 25, 2012. Marauders general manager Trevor Gooby delivered the baby near the ballpark's front gate and the appreciative mother named her newborn son "McKechnie." The High-A Florida State League's Marauders held a "Babies on Deck" game promotion six months later, giving away baby bobbleheads and hosting diaper-changing races between innings.

PUTT PUTT

The Single-A Lansing Lugnuts went from 18 half innings to 18 holes in 2016. The team converted their field to a mini golf course in the off-season.

GRAND SLAMMER

The independent San Rafael Pacifics scheduled a game at a prison as a preseason tune-up in 2012. They played an Inmate All-Star Team at San Quentin State Prison in California. Fans were allowed in, but they were subject to prison visitation policies. Win or lose, the Pacifics got to leave and the long home stand for the Inmate All-Star Team continued.

SWING FOR THE BACKSTOP

The High-A Wilmington Blue Rocks reversed the field for the 2014 California League/Carolina League Home Run Derby. Competitors swung from center field and pelted balls into the seats behind home plate.

STRETCH

When the Single-A Kane County Cougars' bus broke down after a game in Cedar Rapids, Iowa, on August 28, 2014, the team arranged for limousines to pick up players and drive them back to the hotel.

NO NEWS IS GOOD NEWS

In 2016, the High-A Lynchburg Hillcats held a name-the-team vote and the choices for their new moniker included Lamb Chops, Love Apples, and River Runners. A few weeks later, the club announced they were sticking with Hillcats.

AN APPROPRIATE TEAM NAME

There's a tower near the Lansing Lugnuts' ballpark with what is promoted as "the world's largest lugnut" attached to its roof.

FLOODED

With both dugouts at Kentucky's Bowling Green Ballpark submerged in water from an afternoon rainstorm on August 6, 2016, Single-A Bowling Green Hot Rods and West Michigan Whitecaps players sat in the stands during the game.

VAGABONDS

The Double-A Hartford Yard Goats played the entire 2016 season, all 141 games, on the road because of their new stadium's construction delays.

POSTPONED BY VOLCANO

The Triple-A Spokane Indians didn't play on May 18, 1980, because their field was covered in ash from the eruption of Mount St. Helens earlier that day.

WHERE TO?

The Everett AquaSox and Spokane Indians played a Northwest League playoff game at Seattle's Safeco Field on September 9, 2016, because Everett's complex was being used for high school football and Spokane's park was booked by a county fair.

URINE SECOND PLACE

The Triple-A Lehigh Valley IronPigs' ballpark bathrooms finished second in the 2016 America's Best Restroom competition. The IronPigs became a finalist after installing screens above their urinals that, as the team announced, presented "p-controlled video game systems" that were "sure to make a huge splash."

NOTHING BUT NET

The High-A Florida State League's Charlotte Stone Crabs postponed their home game on May 22, 2017, because their backstop netting couldn't get repaired in time after Jupiter catcher Roy Morales fell into it while making a catch a few days before.

THE GEORGIA PEACH

Lake Olmstead Stadium hosted minor league games in Augusta, Georgia, from 1995–2017. The section of outfield fence that was 366 feet from home plate displayed ".366 COBB," recognizing the career batting average of former Augusta resident Ty Cobb.

SUN DELAYS

Sam Lynn Ballpark hosted the California League's Bakersfield Blaze until the franchise relocated in 2017. The park was built facing the wrong direction, so the sun faced batters when it was setting early in games. The team tried numerous sun-shielding strategies over the years, like starting night games later and installing a massive wall in left-center field, but occasionally games had to wait through sun delays.

The minor league ballpark in Pittsfield, Massachusetts, has also experienced sun delays.

GREEN MACHINE

The independent Roswell Invaders won three Pecos League championships from 2011–2018. The team wears lime green jerseys and pants, and their home ballpark features green bases.

BUFFALO WINGS

The Triple-A Buffalo Bisons played a series as the "Buffalo Wings" in 2018. Buffalo wings were reportedly invented in Buffalo, New York, in 1964.

SPEAKING OF CHICKEN

The Double-A New Hampshire Fisher Cats transformed into the Manchester Chicken Tenders for one game in 2022. Chicken tenders were first cooked in a diner in Manchester, New Hampshire, in 1974.

AKA

Double-A San Antonio played a doubleheader under two different team names on July 5, 2018. The club wore their usual San Antonio Missions uniforms in Game 1 and dressed as the San Antonio Flying Chanclas in a Hispanic heritage-themed Game 2.

EVENLY MATCHED

San Antonio played Arkansas 620 times before leaving the Texas League in 2018. At that point, their all-time, head-to-head series record was 310-310.

BROKEN BAT HOME RUNS!

The Triple-A Colorado Springs Sky Sox played in the highest-elevated professional baseball stadium in the United States from 1988–2018. At 6,531 feet above sea level, the conditions led to some astonishing home run stories, like how multiple Colorado Springs players hit balls over the fence on swings that broke their bats.

NO, NOT SCRABBLE

The Single-A Delmarva Shorebirds changed their name for one day in 2018 to the Delmarva Scrapple. Scrapple is a type of breakfast meat that's popular in the Mid-Atlantic region. That game's ballpark festivities included a scrapple eating contest, a scrapple carving contest, and a scrapple cook-off.

UPHILL BATTLES

Howard Johnson Field in Johnson City, Tennessee, hosted minor league games from 1957–2019. For many of those years, it had a 15-foot inclining hill in right field. Rio Grande Credit Union Field, home of the Triple-A Albuquerque Isotopes in New Mexico, has a 127-foot wide hill in center field that also slopes upward to the fence.

Nashville right fielders had a scenic overlook from 1901–1963. The ballpark there had a hill sloping up to the right field wall, which was only 262 feet from home plate. Right fielders stood atop the bluff, 22 feet above their teammates, and ran or tumbled down the hill to pursue balls in front of them.

FOUL SMELL IN FOUL TERRITORY

In 2019, the Triple-A Las Vegas Aviators moved into Las Vegas Ballpark, a beautiful stadium with functioning plumbing. In the final years of the old stadium there, Las Vegas players sometimes had to sit on folding chairs in front of the dugout because sewer water leaked under their bench.

HOT SUMMER NIGHTS

Las Vegas Ballpark became the first professional sports venue to use exclusively mesh seats in its seating bowl. The mesh seats are reportedly 40 degrees cooler than plastic seats.

THE PITCH

The independent Pecos League's High Desert Yardbirds played in an Adelanto, California, soccer stadium in 2019. The mostly-grass field didn't have infield dirt or a warning track and used a fiberglass pitcher's mound.

LET ME CHANGE

The High-A Lake Elsinore Storm changed into their Cadejos de Lake Elsinore alternate uniforms during the game on April 11, 2019, giving all Lake Elsinore players a different jersey in the fifth inning than they wore in the fourth.

MUFFIN TOPS

In 2019, the Double-A Binghamton Rumble Ponies played one game as the Binghamton Stud Muffins, which was one of the finalists from the name-the-team process three years earlier. Stud Muffins was a reference to Binghamton, New York's history of carousel horses.

EXTERMINATORS

The Lowell Spinners were the Boston Red Sox affiliate in the New York-Penn League from 1996–2019. In its later years, the club offered Spinners jerseys to any little league team wearing the uniform of the New York Yankees, Boston's rival. The Spinners called it the "Yankees Elimination Project" and dozens of teams made the conversion.

GENERALLY SPEAKING

There was a Double-A team in Mississippi named the Jackson Generals from 1991–1999 and a different Double-A team in Tennessee named the Jackson Generals from 2011–2019.

POOL PARTY

Las Vegas Ballpark has a pool behind the right-center field fence and when the Triple-A Las Vegas Aviators clinched a playoff spot in 2019, their players jumped in the pool fully clothed while holding up beer cans.

THIS FIELD STINKS

NelsonCorp Field in Clinton, Iowa, hosted professional baseball from 1937–2019. Clinton is home to multiple meatpacking plants and the resulting smell is strong, especially during the day. The odor once made a Lansing Lugnuts third baseman queasy during an afternoon game and he vomited on the field.

LOVE SEATS

In 2020, the High-A Hickory Crawdads announced they'd play select games as the Hickory Couch Potatoes. Hickory, North Carolina, is referred to as the "Furniture Capital of the World."

THE BIG EASY

New Orleans hosted Triple-A baseball from 1993–2019 and fans swam there in a pool above the right field wall.

ON THE LOOKOUT

The Chattanooga, Tennessee, police department put out an APB for a stolen mascot on March 30, 2021. A burglar cut the security camera cord at AT&T Field, home of the Double-A Chattanooga Lookouts, then broke into the stadium, mascot-napped Looie the Lookout's costume, and stole merchandise from the team store. Looie turned up at the nearby Tennessee Aquarium and the burglar was arrested.

SMALL FONT

The Single-A Columbia Fireflies put fans' names on their opening night jersey in 2021. Anyone who bought a preseason ticket package had their name printed on every player's jersey. The jerseys were auctioned off for charity after the Fireflies' first home game in Columbia, South Carolina.

THE MAINE COURSES

The Double-A Portland Sea Dogs honored three Maine food traditions in 2022 by playing select games as the Maine Bean Suppahs, the Maine Red Snappers (a red hot dog), and the Maine Whoopie Pies (a dessert).

ROOFMAN

That's the name of a superhero the Triple-A Reno Aces invented. He dresses in black and tosses soft baseballs down to fans from the stadium roof.

FENG SHUI

The visiting clubhouse at Four Winds Field in South Bend, Indiana, had pink walls, pink couches, and pink sinks until recent renovations gave it a more traditional look.

873 LONG DRIVE, ABERDEEN, MD 21001

The Aberdeen IronBirds are owned by Ripken Baseball and when building the ballpark there, the organization picked its street address based on Cal Ripken Jr.'s (8), Cal Ripken Sr.'s (7), and Bill Ripken's (3) uniform numbers.

LIFE SIZE

Each year, the Double-A Harrisburg Senators induct a former player into their Hall of Fame and unveil a bobblehead statue of the honoree at their ballpark. The statues are the same height as the player, so Cliff Floyd's bobblehead stands 6-foot-5.

ISLAND FEVER

Harrisburg's ballpark is on an island in the Susquehanna River. The team has occasionally had to postpone games because of flooding and its mascot, Rascal, is a friendly river monster.

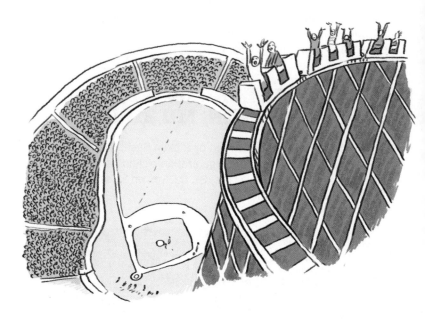

AMUSEMENT PARK

The Skyliner is Lakemont Park's tall rollercoaster located behind the right field wall at the Double-A Altoona Curve's ballpark in Pennsylvania. The rollercoaster is seen by fans at the ballpark and letters spell "Go Curve" on its sides. Riders can look over and watch the game from the moving rollercoaster.

LUCK OF THE DRAW

Nevada's baseball battle is settled each year by the Silver State Diamond Challenge, an annual showdown decided by head-to-head games between the Triple-A Las Vegas Aviators and Reno Aces. If the series ends in a tie, the cities' mayors determine the winner via a card-drawing tiebreaker, in true Nevada fashion.

LIGHT FIXTURE

Cheney Stadium in Tacoma, Washington, still uses the light towers that were transported 770 miles from San Francisco's Seals Stadium in 1960.

STAYCATION

Fans entering North Carolina's McCormick Field, home of the Single-A Asheville Tourists, see a redundant scoreboard. The top line says "Visitors" and the bottom line reads "Tourists."

OUTDOORSY THEME

The Tourists have an enclosed bullpen and their relievers covered the exterior walls with duck blinds during the 2018 season.

McCormick Field also has green hills and trees behind its outfield wall. In recent years, the team hired a company's goats to maintain the area by eating tall grass, and they've had fans zipline from the hills to home plate to deliver first-pitch baseballs before games.

SEAT SAVE

The seats at the Single-A Myrtle Beach Pelicans' ballpark came from Atlanta Fulton County Stadium, former home of MLB's Atlanta Braves.

EAT MY SHORTS

The Triple-A Albuquerque Isotopes got their name, in part, from the episode of *The Simpsons* where Homer is saddened to learn of the Springfield Isotopes' plan to move to Albuquerque, New Mexico. Today fans can see scattered statues of Homer, Marge, Bart, and Lisa Simpson at the Isotopes' ballpark.

MUSIC CITY

First Horizon Park, home of the Triple-A Nashville Sounds, has a 4,200-square-foot guitar-shaped scoreboard behind the right-center field wall.

BILLIONAIRE

Companies can rent Buffett Boardroom at Werner Park, the Triple-A Omaha Storm Chasers' ballpark. The space is named after Warren Buffett, one of the richest people in the world and a former Storm Chasers minority owner. Buffett wore a full baseball uniform when throwing out ceremonial first pitches before Omaha games.

CANNON PUN

The Single-A Kannapolis Cannon Ballers' marketing slogan is "Have a Blast!"

(ROUND) ROCK CLIMBING

Dell Diamond, home of the Triple-A Round Rock Express in Texas, has a full-size rock climbing wall in its fan zone.

SAY IT AIN'T SO

Two Single-A teams in South Carolina have connections to the state's iconic and controversial player, Shoeless Joe Jackson. The Charleston RiverDogs have a sloping seating area called Shoeless Joe's Hill, and the Greenville Drive play across the street from the Shoeless Joe Jackson Museum. Players from the two teams stood on the field in their socks during the national anthem before a recent game as part of a fundraiser to give kids new shoes.

Jackson was one of the best hitters of the early 1900s before he was banned from baseball for participating in the 1919 World Series gambling scandal.

DRINKS AT A DISTANCE

Bar 352, the Double-A Amarillo Sod Poodles' open-air tavern in Texas, sits 352 feet from home plate.

GRANDSTANDER

The Double-A Reading Fightin Phils have a crazy hot dog vendor named "Crazy Hot Dog Vendor." The nightly character rounds the stands on a stuffed ostrich while flinging free hot dogs into the crowd in Reading, Pennsylvania. He wears a paper hat, a bow tie, and thick glasses.

CARNIVAL RIDES

Modern Woodmen Park, home of the High-A Quad Cities River Bandits in Iowa, has a 110-foot-tall Ferris wheel, a carousel, and other amusements.

I CANNOT TELL A LIE

The Single-A Fredericksburg Nationals have a George Washington themed logo and mascot. Fredericksburg, Virginia, is where Washington grew up and where he reportedly cut down a cherry tree and told the truth about doing so.

SHALOM

The High-A South Bend Cubs' team shop is behind the left field fence in a brick building that used to be a historic synagogue that opened in 1901.

TIRED GROUNDSKEEPERS

Roger Dean Stadium in Jupiter, Florida, is the home of two Single-A clubs–the Jupiter Hammerheads and Palm Beach Cardinals. Between their seasons and hosting major league spring training for the Miami Marlins and St. Louis Cardinals, there is a professional baseball game at Roger Dean Stadium about six days a week from late-February to mid-September.

CROSSING STATE LINES

ABC Supply Stadium, home of the High-A Beloit Sky Carp, is in Wisconsin, but foul balls hit over the first base side stands sometimes land on Shirland Avenue and bounce into Illinois.

DUNDER MIFFLIN

The Triple-A Scranton/Wilkes-Barre RailRiders hold *The Office* night at a game each year. The promotion features contests and references connected to the popular show that was set in Scranton, Pennsylvania, and sometimes cast members have appeared.

AIN'T NO PARTY LIKE A SCRANTON PARTY

The RailRiders clinched playoffs spots five years in a row from 2015–2019 and players even slid shirtless on a slip-and-slide during their clubhouse champagne celebrations.

EAT YOUR VEGETABLES

Stockton, California, is the Asparagus Capital of the World, and the Single-A Stockton Ports have asparagus-costumed mascots, sometimes wear asparagus-logoed caps, and sometimes sell asparagus fries, asparagus tacos, and bacon-wrapped asparagus at their concession stands.

BATTERS & RUNNERS

HALF-CREDIT

Former major leaguer Perry Werden claimed he hit a ball so hard in a late 1800s minor league game that the ball split into two pieces. One piece struck a "Hit Me for a Free Pair of Shoes" outfield sign and when Werden arrived to collect his prize, the store owner gave him only one shoe.

SQUANDERED OPPORTUNITY

In 1890, the Anderson club in the Indiana State League hit three triples, a double, and two singles in one inning, but they didn't score any runs. The first two batters tripled and got thrown out trying to score. After a few more hits without a run, the inning ended when a hit struck a runner.

SHORTCUT

Two Oakland Colonels ran directly from second base to home plate during a game against San Francisco in July 1891. The runners got away with the ploy, despite arguments from their opponents, because the game's only umpire was facing first base.

FOUR, TOPS

Dan Cronin hit four home runs in one New England League game, the only four homers of his two-year career. All four long balls cleared the outfield fence in Pawtucket's win over Salem on May 31, 1892.

NAILED IT

A hitter's sharpness and a nail's sharpness gave the Minneapolis Millers an inside-the-park home run in 1898. A Millers batter hammered a pitch to deep center field and the ball got stuck on a wire nail attached to St. Paul's ballpark fence. The batter rounded the bases before a St. Paul outfielder climbed a step ladder and detached the punctured ball.

TWENTY-FOUR INCHES

Andy Oyler hit a two-foot home run in 1905. Oyler was batting for Minneapolis during a soggy home game vs. St. Paul when an inside fastball hit his bat and shot straight down. The ball disappeared in mud two feet in front of home plate and Oyler raced around the bases while St. Paul's fielders searched for it. His two-foot, inside-the-park home run was featured in the children's book *Mudball*.

QUAGMIRE

Eight years later, another Minneapolis batter rounded the bases when his hit got lost in mud. Heinie Berger was batting in Game 2 of a rainy doubleheader on July 17, 1913, and smacked a line drive near second base. The ball disappeared in the waterlogged infield dirt while Berger ran through the rain for an inside-the-park home run.

BLOWN TO SMITHEREENS

Cowboys who had bet money on the game were in the stands for a 1912 Denver vs. St. Joseph Class A matchup in St. Joseph, Missouri. The score was tied in the bottom of the ninth inning with the bases loaded and two outs when St. Joseph's batter lifted a fly ball to center field. With the ball on its way down toward the center fielder, the cowboys pulled out their pistols and shot the ball into bits.

Umpire Steamboat Johnson ruled it a game-ending grand slam since the ball disappeared from his view.

GUTTERBALL

A hitter turned a strikeout into a home run on May 28, 1909, in a Class C Texas League game. A Dallas Giants batter named Overton swung and missed at strike three and when the ball bounced away from the Fort Worth catcher, Overton took off for first base. The catcher was searching for the ball while Overton rounded first, turned at second, and bolted for third. The catcher finally spotted the ball, but it was too late. Overton came around to score while the ball was stuck in a gutter.

SWING AND A MIST

Thick fog at a Class B New England League game in Lynn, Massachusetts, on May 20, 1911, made it so outfielders couldn't see each other. Fall River's Buck Weaver hit a soaring fly ball into the fog and Lynn's outfielders couldn't find the ball when it landed. Weaver rounded the bases for an inside-the-park, or outside-the-park, home run. Nobody knew for sure. The ball was lost.

DODGED A BULLET

The story of the pistol-shooting gamblers wasn't the only time umpire Steamboat Johnson faced gunfire in the early 1900s. A mob of fans chased him after a game in Atlanta because of a contested call and he made it to his locker room safely, but one of the angry fans shot at him while he was showering. The bullet missed him because he was bending down to wash his feet.

FROM BEYOND THE GRAVE

Heinie Heitmuller won the 1912 Pacific Coast League batting title a month after he died. Heitmuller caught typhoid fever on September 29 and had to leave the team. At the time of his departure, his .335 average was second-best in the league, three points away from the league leader. Heitmuller's health worsened and he passed away on October 8, with enough plate appearances to qualify for the batting title. The league leader slumped in the season's final three weeks, so Heitmuller's .335 finished as the top batting average.

PAT ON THE BACK

Wausau Lumberjacks batter Mike Cavanaugh hit a home run on opening day in the Class C Wisconsin-Illinois League in 1914 but was called out because his third base coach ran on the field and slapped him on the back with excitement.

DRESS BLUES

A Rhode Island clothing store offered a free suit to the Providence Grays player who stole the most bases in 1917. Fred Brainard led the team in steals but was in the army at the time of the suit presentation, so the store made him a soldier's uniform and shipped it to his base.

DUST UP

Jersey City Skeeters runner Al Schacht made a baseball disappear in a cloud of dust. Schacht dove into first base on a pickoff throw in 1919, rolled onto the ball, and slipped it into his pocket. As Buffalo's first baseman scrambled in the cloud of dust looking for the ball, Schacht ran around the bases and scored. When Schacht slid home, the stolen baseball popped out of his pocket. He was called out and fined $50.

INTERCEPTION

Greenwood Indians outfielder Charles Bell was frustrated one day during a 1922 Class D Cotton States League game because an opposing pitcher kept throwing him slow curveballs. During his fourth at bat, Bell took one hand off his bat, reached out, caught the pitcher's next curveball, tossed the ball in the air, swung his bat, and hit a ground ball to shortstop. The umpire ruled the batter's bare-hand stunt a groundout.

LYING IN THE WEEDS

Charleston Pals first baseman Ernie Walker hit an inside-the-park home run against Augusta in a Class B South Atlantic League game on September 3, 1922, when the ball got lost in the tall left field grass.

TRACTORS PLOWED

The Class B Springfield Senators beat the Peoria Tractors 56-23 in Illinois on July 20, 1926.

THEY PUT UP 40!

Here are some other astonishing scores from minor league history: Albuquerque beat El Paso 45-13 on opening day in 1932, and St. Paul defeated Minneapolis 41-8 on July 5, 1896.

YOU CAN'T PREDICT BALL

The New Orleans Pelicans beat the Nashville Vols 32-0 in Game 1 of a Southern Association doubleheader on May 6, 1945. New Orleans was held to one run in Game 2, losing 3-1.

BRUISED BLOOMINGTON BLOOMER

In 1927, Hap Fitzgerald of the Class B Bloomington Bloomers got hit by a pitch in six consecutive plate appearances.

INDELIBLE INNING

The only player in baseball history to hit three home runs in one inning stood just 5-foot-6. Gene "Half Pint" Rye went deep three times in the eighth inning of Class A Waco's 20-7 Texas League win over Beaumont on August 6, 1930. Rye later played in 17 major league games and never hit a home run.

IT LOOKED REAL

San Diego Padres player Del Ballinger found a toy cap gun before the game on June 21, 1946, and put it in his pocket when he came up to pinch-hit in the eighth inning that day. Umpire Gordon Ford called a strike on Ballinger, prompting Ballinger to pull out the gun, press it against Ford's throat, and pull the trigger. Ford was frightened and he ejected Ballinger.

The gun stunt wasn't Ballinger's only prank on umpires. He attached a piece of green string to a baseball, purposely threw the ball past his pitcher during warm-ups, and every time the base umpire bent down to pick up the ball, Ballinger yanked the string, pulled the ball away, and got laughs from players and fans.

CHEAPIES

Lowell Lauriers slugger Larry Donovan hit 20 home runs in 1933 and all 20 homers came in home games. The Lauriers' ballpark in Massachusetts was only 275 feet to the right field wall and only 310 feet to center.

ONE HOP

Class C Amsterdam Rugmakers catcher Ken Sears hit a home run in 1938 on a curveball that bounced on home plate.

MISS-ED IT

A batter struck out twice in a row in 1939. Walter Missler of the Class D Ohio State League's Lima Pandas took a 2-2 pitch and went to the dugout to change bats. Missler didn't realize the umpire had called the pitch strike three when he returned with his new bat. Meanwhile, the umpire thought Missler was Lima's next hitter. After Missler struck out again, the umpire realized his lapse but called two outs against Lima anyway.

BACKSWING BASH

Ed Stewart injured himself in the batter's box. The Class B Vancouver Capilanos hitter swung and missed at a pitch during a 1939 game and the bat whipped around his shoulder and slammed him on the back of the head. He wasn't wearing a helmet and was knocked unconscious.

LOOSE GRIP

Shreveport Sports hitter Vernon Washington accidentally threw his bat into the crowd so frequently in the early 1940s in Shreveport, Louisiana, that the team raised temporary netting in front of the first base stands every time he came to the plate.

STAN THE MAN

A Class D pitcher's shoulder injury helped the St. Louis Cardinals become a dominant team in the 1940s. Hall of Famer Stan Musial pitched for three seasons in the minor leagues and played outfield when he wasn't on the mound. On August 11, 1940, Musial jammed his shoulder trying to make a diving catch for the Daytona Beach Islanders. The busted shoulder made the Cardinals move Musial to the outfield full-time. He became one of the best hitters in MLB history and led the Cardinals to three World Series championships.

12-for-12

The Adams brothers had a day to write home about in 1941. Dick Adams went 6-for-6 in a Class C Fresno Cardinals game and was so excited that he penned a letter to his brother Bobby, an infielder with the Class B Columbia Reds. Bobby also went 6-for-6 that day, and also wrote his brother about it. Both received the letters a few days later.

HOLE IN ONE

In 1942, a Milwaukee Brewers batter hit a low line drive that bounced down the right field line. He rounded the bases while confused Louisville Colonels fielders searched for the ball. They eventually found it inside a gopher hole.

TIMBER!

Class C Winston-Salem Cardinals slugger Steve Bilko chopped down a branch with one home run swing in 1947. Bilko rocked a home run over the center field fence in Winston-Salem, North Carolina, and the ball smashed into a tree, broke off a branch, and dropped two tree-sitting kids to the ground.

TIRE SWING

Al Meau hit a home run in 1947 that paid his rent for the entire season. Bluefield, Virginia's Bowen Field had a hanging tire behind the right field fence and the Class D Bluefield Blue-Grays offered $100 to anyone who hit a home run through the tire. Meau's dinger squeaked through, earning him the boosted paycheck. It was his only career homer.

WALK-KOFF HOME RUN

Lou Novikoff's home run trot became a home run crawl on June 22, 1947. After Novikoff hit a game-ending dinger for the Seattle Rainiers, he rounded third base, dropped to his knees, crawled home, and kissed home plate.

PHIPPS' LIPS

Jodie Phipps showed similar affection for the plate. He pitched in the minor leagues from 1939-1957 and kissed home plate after all 275 of his wins.

LODGED

Kansas City Blues base runner Leon Culberson was given credit for a stolen base by the official scorer after he advanced when a pitch got stuck in the umpire's mask on July 7, 1948. The umpire said it was a live ball, even though he couldn't immediately pry it from his mask.

UNCONSCIOUS RUN

Bob Bundy of the Hollywood Stars tried to score on a sacrifice fly on March 28, 1950, but was knocked out cold in a collision with Portland's catcher. Hollywood's on-deck hitter, Murray Franklin, lifted up Bundy's hand and placed it on home plate. The run counted.

BREAKING AND ENTERING

On August 26, 1950, Spider Jorgensen hit a game-ending home run for Triple-A Minneapolis and the ball soared out of the park, smashed through an appliance shop's window, and set off the burglar alarm.

A home run went into a home in the mid-1950s. Los Angeles Angels slugger Buzz Clarkson blasted a line drive that flew over the left field fence and burst through the front door of a house in Los Angeles. Residents fled the house, fearful that they were under attack.

OVERDRESSED

The Triple-A San Francisco Seals started wearing collars on their jerseys in 1950. Seals leadoff hitter Jack Tobin was so excited about the new look that he came to the plate wearing a bow tie. The umpire made Tobin remove it.

POWER NAP

In 1951, Nashville's Babe Barna lined a home run in Birmingham, Alabama, that flew over the right field fence and hit a fan who was sleeping in the bleachers.

BATTING AROUND AND AROUND AND AROUND

In the fifth inning of their 30-4 win over Wilson on June 2, 1951, the Class D Coastal Plain League's Tarboro Serpents sent 25 batters to the plate before making an out. The inning finally ended after 24 runs and 29 hitters.

SOLO HOMER

Ralph "Froggie" Betcher stepped to the plate on July 3, 1952, and hit a home run for the Cordele A's, the only homer Cordele hit all season. The team had 22 players, 139 games, 4,679 at bats, and only one home run. Dozens of individual players in the Class D Georgia-Florida League out-homered the A's that season.

BOLD BASERUNNING

The Western League's Pueblo Dodgers stole home three times in a three-pitch span on July 16, 1952. Danny Hayling was the batter for all three risky runs.

NONSMOKING SECTION

The Southern Association's Chattanooga Lookouts lost a playoff game in 1952 because a runner called time to give his first base coach a pack of cigarettes. It was a tie score in the bottom of the ninth inning, and a Memphis pitcher threw a wild pitch to bring in the winning run from third base. But the Lookouts' runner at first had asked for time so he could give the first base coach his cigarettes to hold. The runner who scored had to return to third, and Chattanooga didn't score again. Memphis won the game and the series.

HOME RUN RERUN

A Double-A Texas League player hit back-to-back home runs with himself on May 29, 1955. Fort Worth's eighth batter Joe Pignatano incorrectly came up in the seventh spot and hit a home run. After being called out for batting out of order, he stepped into the box again and hit another home run.

OVER/UNDER

Joe Tipton was banned from baseball for hitting too many foul balls. While playing for the Southern Association's Birmingham Barons in 1957, Tipton communicated with gamblers in the stands, who were betting on how long each at bat would last. Tipton was paid by the gamblers to intentionally foul off pitches and rig the betting results.

NO PEPPER GAMES

Pepper Martin is reportedly the oldest pinch runner in baseball history. Martin, the 1930s MLB All-Star, was coaching for the Double-A Tulsa Oilers at age 54 in 1958 when he pinch-ran for a pitcher.

FOUNTAIN OF FUROR

Larry Segovia went to bat on a clear night and three strikes later people were soaking wet. The Class B Albuquerque Dukes outfielder struck out on June 15, 1955, in Pampa, Texas, and after the K he stormed into the dugout and kicked a water fountain. His kick broke a pipe and water gushed out, spraying everyone in sight. The geyser soared 50 feet high, drenching players and fans. The game was delayed as the grounds crew shut off the water and cleaned puddles off the field.

RUNNING LAPS

Las Vegas Wranglers infielder Elmo Plaskett jogged around the bases twice after his home run in Fresno, California, on August 10, 1958. Plaskett missed first base the first time around, so he ran around the bases again, stepping on each base during the second go-around. Fresno appealed and Plaskett was called out for missing first the first time.

650 FEET!

Carlsbad Potashers slugger Gil Carter turned on a fastball on August 11, 1959, in Carlsbad, New Mexico, and reportedly pulverized it 650 feet. The ball soared over the left field wall, flew out of the stadium, and rolled through a neighborhood before finally stopping 733 feet from home plate. Carter's strapping power partnered with hitter-friendly conditions that night–it was roasting hot and Carlsbad is 3,300 feet above sea level. A fan returned the ball to Carter and it rested on his mantel until his death in 2015.

HARMFUL IF SWALLOWED

Albuquerque Dodgers batter Cleo James had to leave a Double-A Texas League playoff game in 1965 after one pitch because he became sick from accidentally swallowing a mouthful of chewing tobacco.

STUMP SPEECH

Former New York Yankees manager Stump Merrill likes to tell the story of his half-hour at bat in 1971. He was batting for the Triple-A Eugene Emeralds in Eugene, Oregon, when the ballpark was evacuated because of a bomb threat. After a 30-minute security delay, Merrill came back up and struck out.

SKIPPER

Years later, Merrill was managing the Double-A Trenton Thunder and spent a season living on a boat on the Delaware River.

A ROUND-TRIPPER TRIP & FALL

For most players, their first Double-A home run is a great memory. For Steve Turigliatto, it resulted in a hospital visit. The Dallas-Fort Worth Spurs catcher went deep in a Dixie Association game on August 15, 1971, but he fell down while running the bases and broke his elbow. Turigliatto got up and finished his home run trot, but he didn't play again that season because of the injury.

BLINDED BY THE LIGHT

Florida State League hitters dreaded traveling to Winter Haven in the 1970s because of dim lighting in the ballpark. One night in 1975, the visiting Tampa Tarpons' leadoff hitter walked to the plate with a flashlight taped to the top of his helmet. The umpire noticed the hitter's practical joke and ejected him.

LONGEST HOME RUN EVER

Toledo's Randy Bush hit a home run that traveled 200 miles on April 14, 1982. The Triple-A Toledo Mud Hens were on the road in Charleston, West Virginia, when Bush smacked a homer over the right field fence. The ball landed in a moving coal train, which didn't stop until hours later.

POWER LINE DRIVE

Double-A San Antonio's Jerry Reed stopped a game with one swing on August 11, 1976. Reed hit a foul ball that split a power line in El Paso, Texas. The ballpark lost electricity and the game was suspended in the seventh inning.

UNLIKE FATHER, UNLIKE SON

Hank Aaron's son Lary played two seasons in the minors in the early 1980s and hit only one home run.

AIR JORDAN ETIQUETTE

The Double-A Huntsville Stars got mad at Birmingham's Michael Jordan for stealing a base when his team had a big lead late in a 1994 Southern League game, so Jordan apologized to Huntsville manager Gary Jones the next day and autographed a basketball for him.

DEMOLITION DARYLE

Double-A Jackson Generals slugger Daryle Ward hit a ball through the right field fence at Smith-Wills Stadium in Jackson, Mississippi, in April 1997. The foul line drive flew 325 feet and burst through the wall, leaving a baseball-sized hole.

EXTRA POINT

The score was tied 20-20 and Arkansas Travelers batter Tyrone Horne needed only one pitch to end a wild Double-A Texas League game on June 15, 1998. Horne belted a walk-off home run in the bottom of the tenth inning against Jackson, giving the Travelers a 21-20 victory.

MANNY BEING MANNY

In 2002, Boston Red Sox star Manny Ramirez was playing a Triple-A injury rehab game for Pawtucket in Syracuse, New York, when he lost his diamond earring sliding into third base. He found the earring's stud after the game, but the $15,000 diamond was lost forever.

BLACK DIAMOND

The Nashua Pride's offense went downhill when Olympic skier Bode Miller joined the club in publicity stunts. Miller signed three different one-day contracts and played one game per year from 2006–2008. He went a combined 0-for-6 with five strikeouts.

INTERMISSION

The 2006 Double-A Southern League All-Star Game in Montgomery, Alabama, included a home run derby after the bottom of the third inning. Jacksonville's Craig Brazell beat Chattanooga's Joey Votto and then the game resumed.

OPEN HOUSE

A real estate agent won the 2007 Triple-A Home Run Derby in Albuquerque, New Mexico. Rob Stratton, a realtor and former Albuquerque Isotopes slugger, was invited to participate in the event. He finished first, ahead of active players.

GET AN ESTIMATE

Drew Macias damaged his relationship with an umpire. Macias was playing for Triple-A Portland in Salt Lake City in 2009 when he hooked a foul ball over the stands and into the parking lot, where it smashed the windshield of the umpire's car.

That's not as bad as Gateway Grizzlies batter Brandon Thomas, whose grand slam on August 21, 2016, in Sauget, Illinois, flew into the players' parking lot and smashed his own truck's windshield.

BLAZING SPEED

Stuntman Ted Batchelor ran the bases while on fire after the Single-A Savannah Sand Gnats game on August 10, 2010. Heat stunts are Batchelor's specialty–he once set a world record for being on fire for the longest period of time.

RECYCLED

Tyler Colvin's cycle didn't last long. Colvin hit a single, double, triple, and home run for the Triple-A Iowa Cubs in Albuquerque, New Mexico, on June 17, 2011, but the official scorer changed the single to an Albuquerque fielding error after the game, nullifying the cycle.

SHARING IS CARING

The Boise Hawks lost their batting helmets before their road game against the Spokane Indians on August 18, 2011, in Spokane, Washington, and had to borrow the Indians' helmets. Boise's helmets later turned up on the team bus. The players forgot them when unloading at the ballpark.

BASEBALL BEDLAM

The 2012 Double-A Eastern League Home Run Derby at Pennsylvania's FirstEnergy Stadium, home of the Reading Phillies, had dunk tanks, trampolines, and fans on the field in a protected "VIP Infield Party." Batters gained extra points for striking flamingo lawn ornaments, and team mascots zigzagged through the outfield, lunging and diving for batted balls. Grammy Award-winner David Cullen performed behind a screen on the pitcher's mound as line drives whizzed over his head.

SA-NO YOU DON'T

Miguel Sano went deep and then went home for the High-A Fort Myers Miracle on April 21, 2013. His home run came three pitches after a Palm Beach Cardinals pitcher fired a fastball behind Sano's head. Sano was ejected while rounding the bases for shouting at the pitcher and the Palm Beach dugout during his home run trot. The run counted and he left the game after touching home plate.

AUTOMATIC SINGLE

Double-A Mississippi Braves catcher Christian Bethancourt bounced a hit over the left field fence on June 10, 2013, but he was held at first base. The hit came with the bases loaded and the score tied in the bottom of an extra inning. When the runner from third scored, the game ended, and the official scorer gave Bethancourt a single.

THE ONE-PITCH STRIKEOUT

Double-A Midland's Vinnie Catricala took a called strike on August 1, 2013, in Corpus Christi, Texas, and stepped out of the box to argue. The umpire thought he was taking too much time, so he called an automatic strike two on him. When Catricala argued that call, the umpire called an automatic strike three and ejected him.

COMEBACK?

The Milwaukee Brewers sent assistant hitting coach Jason Lane up to bat in an exhibition game against their Double-A affiliate in Biloxi, Mississippi, on April 2, 2016, and Lane hit a home run.

CIRIACO & CIRIACO

There were two Juan Ciriacos in the Sacramento vs. Albuquerque Triple-A box score on May 3, 2016. Juan Ciriaco batted eighth and played second base for Sacramento and his brother Juan Ciriaco batted eighth and played second base for Albuquerque. They have another brother named Juan, which is also their father's name.

WORST PERFORMANCE EVER?

On May 15, 2016, Single-A Hickory first baseman Dylan Moore went 0-for-8 in a 19-inning home game against Rome. When his team ran out of pitching, Moore moved from first base to the mound and allowed seven runs to lose the game.

A CYCLE FOR CYCLES

After Triple-A Albuquerque Isotopes teammates Tom Murphy and Pat Valaika both hit for the cycle in the summer of 2016, the team had them hop on a tandem bike and ride it around the warning track before a game while being taped by a TV station.

Speaking of teammate cycles, it had been almost a decade since the California League's San Jose Giants had a player hit for the cycle when both Gio Brusa and Jalen Miller did it in the same game for San Jose on April 11, 2018.

SPLASHING HOMERS

The 2016 California League vs. Carolina League All-Star Game Home Run Derby was held on the deck of the *USS Midway*, a 64,000-ton aircraft carrier in San Diego. Fans huddled around a batting cage and behind a fence to watch players smash home runs into the Pacific Ocean.

NOT A REPLAY

Some teams go an entire season without hitting a home run off a foul pole. The Triple-A Toledo Mud Hens hit back-to-back homers off the left field foul pole in a home win over Louisville on May 17, 2017.

SHIRT SWAP

Single-A Wisconsin's Monte Harrison hit a home run in the 2017 Midwest League All-Star Game, reached first base, took off his jersey, gave it to his first base coach, took his first base coach's jersey, ran to second base without a shirt on, put the coach's jersey on, reached home plate, and took a selfie with teammates.

GRAB A LADDER

High-A Buies Creek Astros hitter Randy Cesar swung and missed, lost control of the bat, and flung it onto Grainger Stadium's roof in Kinston, North Carolina, on August 18, 2017.

CALL LOUIE'S FLOOR COVERING IN DES MOINES

When Triple-A Iowa's David Bote hit a ball over Oklahoma City's left fielder's head on April 5, 2018, fans were confused. Nobody saw it clear the fence, but after a pause, they began cheering as if it were a home run. The ball had actually slipped behind a banner attached to the left field wall and went for a ground-rule double.

FOUR RUNNERS, ONE PITCH

The Northwest League's Hillsboro Hops started their bottom of the eleventh inning on July 14, 2018, with an automatic runner at second base, then hit a first-pitch triple, then had two players given automatic intentional walks. Four different base runners reached base and there was only one pitch thrown.

WIDESPREAD PANIK

San Francisco Giants infielder Joe Panik played for two different teams in two different leagues on July 30, 2018. Panik had two injury rehab at bats in Triple-A Sacramento's home day game, flew to San Diego, got activated from the injured list, and went 0-for-1 as a pinch hitter in that night's Giants road game.

Alex Herrnberger knows the feeling. He batted for two different teams in two different cities on August 3, 2010. He pinch-hit for the Arizona Diamondbacks' Triple-A affiliate, the Reno Aces, in their day game in Tacoma, Washington, then boarded a prop plane and flew to join the D-backs' short-season affiliate in Yakima, Washington, where he played in their home game that night.

PERFECT SHOT

When Triple-A El Paso's Brett Nicholas struck out swinging during a 2018 road game against the Iowa Cubs, he accidentally let the bat go at the end of his swing. The bat twisted through the air and into the first base dugout, where it dropped into his team's bat rack.

DON'T BREAK IT

All Single-A Carolina Mudcats batters shared one bat on the final day of both the 2017 and 2021 seasons. They won both games.

BEACON

Maine is known for its lighthouses and the Double-A Portland Sea Dogs have one behind their center field fence. It shoots off pyrotechnics whenever Sea Dogs batters hit a home run.

PITCHERS & FIELDERS

TOMATO SAUCE

Davenport's Jack Fanning pitched a 19-0 no-hitter over Springfield on September 15, 1889, in Davenport, Iowa. After the game, 200 Davenport fans picked ripe tomatoes from a nearby field and threw them at the departing Springfield players. Police came to break up the ensuing fight between the players and fans.

ILL-SUITED

The Canton Nadjys sent a 23-year-old pitcher to Cleveland for $250 and a new suit in 1890. The pitcher was future all-time wins leader Cy Young.

AN APPLE A DAY

First baseman Tacks Parrott tried to eat an apple while playing during an early 1900s minor league game. When the ball came toward him, he tossed the apple aside. A confused base runner thought the apple was the ball and kept running until Parrott threw him out.

QUICKSTEPS? MORE LIKE MISSTEPS

The Paris Quicksteps of Paris, Texas, made 34 errors in a 31-29 win in 1884. The Quicksteps played barehanded and wore cowboy boots on the field.

TAKE A BREAK

The Kentucky-Illinois-Tennessee League had a restful right fielder one day in the early 1900s. The player was tired from chasing many long hits, so he asked if he could lay on the outfield grass for two minutes. The umpire said yes, and fans stood up and stretched during the rest time.

CRAPSHOOTER

Early 1900s pitcher Elmer Koestner was known for his frequent visits to casinos. One day, while pitching for the Pacific Coast League's Venice Tigers, Koestner tripped on the mound and several dice fell out of his pants pocket.

FIELD DRESSING

Pitcher Carl Zamloch was the son of famous magician "Zamloch the Great," and Carl made the middle of a baseball disappear during an early 1900s Pacific Coast League game. He cut a ball open, removed the inside materials, and took the ball's cover with him to the mound. Later in the game, he put the empty cover in his glove so it looked like a real ball. Meanwhile, his second baseman held the game ball and tagged out an opposing base runner.

MASK MEETS MELON

In the early 1900s, a catcher knocked himself out during a Class D Kentucky-Illinois-Tennessee League game in Hopkinsville, Kentucky. The catcher tossed his mask in the air when pursuing a pop-up, and the mask came down and landed on his head, knocking him out cold.

CAN'T GET NO RELIEF

The Texas League's Corsicana Oil Citys didn't use any relief pitchers in 1902.

COMBINATION PUNCH

Schenectady Frog Alleys catcher Dan Coogan was mad after a call at third base during a 1903 Class B New York State League game, so he swatted the umpire's hat off and punched him in the ribs. Coogan was ejected.

POCKET CHANGE

The Class C Jacksonville Jays released a pitcher in 1904 when the dimes and nickels he stole while taking tickets earlier in the day fell out of his socks and onto the field during the game.

NOCTAMBULATION

Class A Montgomery Senators pitcher Duke Carter broke his arm on July 16, 1904, when he fell out of a hotel's third-story window while sleepwalking.

POPCORN ON THE COBB

Future Hall of Famer Ty Cobb was playing left field for the Class C Augusta Tourists on opening day in 1905 when he missed a fly ball because he was eating popcorn.

QUARTER POUNDER

Pitcher C. C. Hodge's contract was purchased for 25 cents by the Class D Holyoke Paperweights in 1906.

LOST AT SEA

The Class A Buffalo Bisons finished a road trip in Providence, Rhode Island, in May 1906 and boarded a steamship for overnight travel to New York City. Bisons pitcher Bill Thomas disappeared from the boat and was never seen again.

EXPANDING THE ZONE

In 1936, Class B Durham Bulls pitcher Johnny Vander Meer was having difficulty throwing strikes over the outside corner to right-handed batters, so he broke into the ballpark at midnight with the groundskeeper, dug up home plate, and moved it three inches toward first base. Nobody noticed and Vander Meer got more outside-corner strike calls in his next few home starts.

UNDER FIRE

Class B Waterbury's combined no-hitter over New London on June 2, 1906, in Waterbury, Connecticut, was interrupted by a fire under the grandstand in the eighth inning. Nobody was hurt and the game continued.

THE FUGITIVE

Columbia's Robert Wallace was ejected from a Class C South Atlantic League game on June 28, 1906, for cursing at the umpire. When Wallace refused to leave the field, the umpire summoned three nearby police officers. Wallace took off and hopped over the outfield fence to avoid the cops. He was eventually apprehended and brought to jail.

HOT POTATO

Double-A Williamsport Bills catcher Dave Bresnahan threw a potato down the left field line on August 28, 1987. With a Reading Phillies runner at third base, Bresnahan asked for time, jogged to the dugout, and grabbed a new glove with a peeled potato hidden in it. As the next pitch came in, Bresnahan transferred the potato to his throwing hand, caught the pitch, and whipped the potato past third base. Reading's runner raced home and was baffled when Bresnahan tagged him out. Bresnahan was released the next day because of the potato prank.

SOX PITCHER

In 1907, Class A Nashville Volunteers pitcher Hub Perdue pitched a game in his socks.

NO SHOES, NO SOCKS, NO PROBLEM

Marlin Stuart did one better than Hub Perdue and pitched a complete game barefoot in 1940. The Class D Mayfield Browns' righty got management's permission to perform the shoeless stunt and went the distance in Mayfield's 5-2 win. Stuart later pitched six years in the majors, where he wore cleats.

UPLIFTING

Tall Jersey City first baseman George Merritt lifted short Newark base runner Jim Cockman on July 4, 1907, and dropped him in the baseline between first and second during a Class A Eastern League game. Merritt then got the ball and tagged Cockman before he could get back to the base. The umpire missed Merritt's move and called Cockman out.

DEFENSIVE METRICS

Class D Oshkosh Indians owner J. M. Sawyer and his wife felt their outfielders stood around and did nothing, so they told manager Kid Nichols to use a seven-man infield, leaving the outfield vacant. The experiment ended during its first game in 1908 when an umpire ordered the fielders to return to their typical positions.

ERROR IN JUDGEMENT

Marion Diggers shortstop Frank Wolfe was arrested on September 3, 1908, for assaulting the official scorer after a Class D Ohio State League game. Wolfe disagreed with the scorer's decision to charge him with an error that day.

NO-HITTER HOMER

A Class B pitcher threw a no-hitter despite allowing a home run on September 16, 1908. Vancouver's George Engle surrendered a long ball to Seattle's Ralph Kreitz in the second inning, but Kreitz somehow missed both first and third base during his home run trot and the umpire called him out. Engle didn't allow any hits before or after Kreitz's "run."

LONGEST NO-HITTER

Fred Toney pitched a 17-inning no-hitter on May 10, 1909, for the Class D Winchester Hustlers of the Blue Grass League. It's still the longest no-hitter in professional baseball history.

FURLOUGHED

In 1931, Sacramento Senators pitcher Tony Freitas was given a five-day jail sentence for multiple speeding tickets. Freitas convinced the judge to let him pitch in a road game in San Francisco and then return to jail.

DOUBLE NO-HITTERS

There have been at least 10 games in minor league history in which neither team got a hit.

LIVE STREAMING

In 1910, future Hall of Famer Casey Stengel played for the Class D Maysville Rivermen in Kentucky and one day the man met the river. There was a deep fly ball heading toward a nearby stream and Stengel chased it, splashed ankle deep in water, and caught the ball.

SLOW DAY AT THE OFFICE

Class D Shelbyville Rivermen outfielders didn't touch the ball in their game in Kentucky against Winchester on July 21, 1910. All hits and outs went to Shelbyville infielders that day.

DRINKING ON THE JOB

In the 1910s, Class B Galveston Pirates pitcher Gene "Blue Goose" Moore got his nickname from visiting the Blue Goose Saloon for pregame shots after retrieving batting practice home run balls that rolled near the saloon.

FLIPPY

A circus acrobat-turned-outfielder tumbled into an unassisted triple play on July 19, 1911. Class A Vernon Tigers center fielder Walter Carlisle raced in pursuing a line drive when he noticed two base runners had taken off trying to steal. Carlisle, who also worked as a circus performer, caught the ball while somersaulting and continued to the infield, where he stepped on second base for the second out. He then tagged the runner lingering between first and second for the third out.

TAKE THE STAND

Class B Lowell Grays catcher Harry Huston witnessed a murder in Ohio weeks before the 1912 season. He wasn't able to report to Lowell, Massachusetts, because the Ohio court ordered him to testify in the murder trial, so the Grays traded him to the Class B Zanesville Potters in Ohio.

LAWN CLIPPINGS

Newark Indians pitcher Al Schacht was fined for crawling around the infield and eating grass during an International League game in the 1910s.

BEER LEAGUE

Future Hall of Famer Rube Waddell played for Class A
Minneapolis in 1911 and had a clause in his contract that
he had to remain sober to get paid. He didn't get paid for
the final game of the season because, while playing right
field, he brought a keg of beer and a chair into the field
with him.

TWO-TIMING

A catcher named Taylor took one for the team, well, both teams, on June 11, 1912. Taylor was the starting catcher for the Class D Yazoo City Zoos in a Cotton States League doubleheader that day against the Columbus Joy Riders. The Columbus catcher was injured in the second inning of Game 1 and the Joy Riders didn't have a backup to replace him, so Taylor offered to catch for both teams and the umpire agreed to ensure the doubleheader could finish.

Three decades later, Julius Homokay played for both teams in a Class A Eastern League game. He pitched for Waterbury against Utica one day and the game was halted by a manager's protest. Homokay was traded from Waterbury to Utica before the game resumed weeks later, and he pitched in the resumption against his old team.

RAILROADED

A train schedule helped John Frill pitch a perfect game on July 6, 1912. Frill's Jersey City Skeeters and their opponent, the Providence Grays, agreed to shorten their game to seven innings as a gesture to the umpire, who had to leave early to catch a train. Frill threw seven perfect innings, a perfect game that's still listed in the International League record book.

TRAINED HANDS

The best minor league catch in 1912 came from a gloveless driver on July 17. A train was traveling by Eclipse Park in Louisville, Kentucky, at 45 mph when a foul ball whizzed past the stands toward the front of the train. Engineer William Madden leaned out the window and caught the ball with his bare hands and the crowd roared with delight. He threw the ball back and it landed in the outfield.

CAREER CHANGE

J.B. Gentle pitched for the Class D Valdosta Millionaires in 1913 then quit to become a Georgia State League umpire.

It was the opposite path of South Texas League umpire Wilson Matthews, who resigned during the 1903 Galveston vs. San Antonio playoff series to join Galveston's roster as a player.

DON'T KNOW NO-NO

On-field updates traveled slower before broadcasts, scoreboards, and tweets. At the conclusion of Lefty Miller's no-hitter for the Class D Central Association's Burlington Pathfinders in 1914, the fans in Burlington, Iowa, were calm because they didn't realize it was a no-hitter. Burlington's mayor walked onto the field, faced the crowd, announced the historic details, and the fans went wild.

LONG TOSS

Montreal Royals pitcher Bob Couchman had a rough outing against Toronto on June 11, 1914, and his manager started walking out to remove him from the game with the bases loaded. The hurler was furious about being taken out, so he turned and threw the ball over the outfield wall. But time hadn't been called, the ball was live, and the umpires allowed all three runners to score.

JAIL-BYRD

Phoenix Senators catcher Byrd Lynn was arrested during a 1915 Class D Rio Grande Association game in El Paso, Texas, for breaking umpire Harry Kane's toe. Lynn was so upset about a ninth-inning call that he threw his bat at Kane. The bat struck Kane in the foot and broke his big toe.

UP AGAINST A WALL

A storm knocked down the Class D Martinsburg Mountaineers' outfield fence in 1920 and the team used their prospect pitcher to pay for a new one. The Mountaineers agreed to send Lefty Grove to the International League's Baltimore Orioles if the Orioles bought them a new outfield fence. The Orioles agreed and Grove went on to win 300 major league games with the Philadelphia Athletics and Boston Red Sox.

MUGGING THE MANAGER

Newark Bears pitcher Ed Tomlin beat up manager Fred Burchell on August 26, 1926, when Burchell removed him from a game. The pitcher was fined $500 and suspended for the rest of the International League season.

THE CHIMNEY SWEEPER

One day around 1920, Louisville Colonels first baseman Jay Kirke arrived at a team meeting in St. Paul, Minnesota, covered in soot and dust. He had climbed into the chimney connected to St. Paul's clubhouse to eavesdrop on his opponents' team meeting.

HOG WILD

Pea Ridge Day bellowed as well as he pitched the 1920s. After each strikeout, the husky flame-throwing journeyman froze on the mound, stared at the batter, and yelled like a hog. Some opponents asked Ridge to put his hog call out to pasture.

SNIPE'S SYMPTOMS

The Wichita Falls Spudders suspected Dallas pitcher Snipe Conley of throwing spitballs during a 1922 game, so they secretly put chemicals on the ball. Conley moved his hand from his mouth to the ball often, so after a few innings his mouth was burning, his tongue was swollen, and he couldn't talk.

SALES PITCH

Bill Sisler pitched for 50 minor league teams and never made it to the majors. He traveled from city to city from 1923–1950, persuading team owners to give him a chance. Oftentimes, he was released after a handful of shaky outings.

DOWN A RUN

Wichita Falls Spudders pitcher Rube Marshall hit a home run in a 1921 Class A Texas League game and was so proud of his dinger that he walked over to the hand-operated scoreboard after an inning, ripped down the wooden number that represented his homer, and kept it as a souvenir.

CAGED MUTT

San Antonio's Mutt Williams won 20 Texas League games in 1921 but team management grew concerned with his heavy drinking. They locked Williams in the ticket booth for a few hours before his starts to make sure he took the mound sober.

WARMING UP

Mutt had an unusual way of loosening up before starts in the 1920s. He lit a piece of paper and swayed it under his pitching arm to heat up, instead of a traditional pregame throwing session.

UNDERHANDED TACTICS

Class C Winston-Salem hurler Thomas Gheen baffled hitters and humored fans with his underhand delivery that produced pitches with great accuracy and puzzling movement. On April 26, 1922, Gheen underhanded his way to a perfect game against Greensboro.

NOT A GOLD GLOVER

Kansas City Blues third baseman Howard Freigau made four errors on one play on July 4, 1927. He bobbled a ground ball for the first error and made a wide throw to first base for the second error. The right fielder picked up the ball and threw it to third base, where Freigau missed the ball for his third error. With the runner trying to score, Freigau picked up the ball and threw it past the catcher for his fourth error.

COMEDY OF ERRORS

Howard Freigau's four-error play was bad, but the Tri-City Atoms' five-error play was even worse. It came at the end of a Northwest League game in 1966 in Eugene, Oregon. Eugene had the bases loaded when the game's final batter hit a grounder to the pitcher, who lobbed the ball over the first baseman's head. The first baseman retrieved the ball and threw it past the catcher, who grabbed the ball at the backstop and fired it into center field, trying to get a runner at second. The center fielder fumbled the ball and launched it over the catcher's head as the batter rounded the bases with the winning run. Tri-City's four throwing errors and one fielding error made for one of the worst defensive sequences in baseball history.

BASEBALL BITES

The Class B Southeastern League's Pensacola Flyers scored four runs on one play in 1928 when a Selma Cloverleafs outfielder tried to eat the ball. Selma center fielder John King dropped a fly ball with the bases loaded and was so upset that he picked up the ball and started eating it. All three runners and the batter scored while King was chomping.

MAGIC BEANS

The Class A Texas League's Wichita Falls Spudders traded pitcher Euel Moore for a plate of beans in 1930.

ARMOR

Pueblo, Colorado's rocky field conditions led to the most heavily-padded infielder in Western League history. Unpredictable ground balls bruised Wichita second baseman Glen McNally early in a 1928 game, so when the third inning started, McNally jogged onto the field wearing shin guards, a chest protector, and a catcher's mask.

AT LEAST THE BALLS WERE NEW

George Hubbell was toiling in the minor leagues at the same time his brother Carl was excelling in the major leagues. George was playing in the Class C Western Association in 1932 and on August 11 he was traded from the Muskogee Chiefs to the Hutchinson Wheat Shockers for four new baseballs.

DRYWALL

A Class A Trenton Senators employee stopped by pitcher Joe Krakauskas's hotel room in 1936 to ask how his arm was feeling. Krakauskas found a baseball, wound up, and fired it through the hotel wall, startling guests in the next room. The team was billed for the wall repair.

JUST A BIT HIGH

Hopkinsville pitcher Johnny Schmitz threw a ball over the backstop in 1938 when the umpire refused to give him a new one. He was ejected.

DENTAL DAMAGE

Joe Sprinz should've worn his catcher's mask. Sprinz, the San Francisco Seals' catcher, tried to catch a baseball dropped 800 feet from a blimp as part of a 1939 baseball event. The ball hit him in the mouth, fractured his jaw, and knocked out eight teeth.

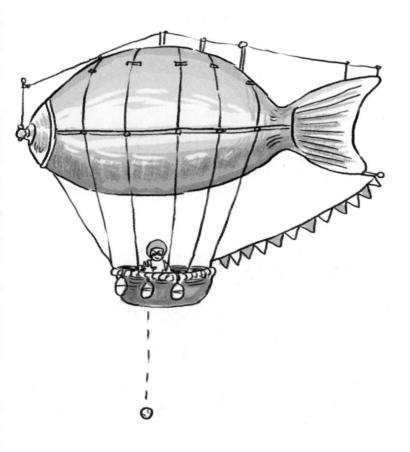

NOT PAYING ATTENTION

In 1940, two runs scored in a Class B Western International League game when Tacoma Tigers catcher Billy Brenner forgot to retrieve a passed ball and stayed crouched behind home plate.

RANGE

Speedy Texarkana Twins center fielder Charlie Metro raced across the outfields of the Class C East Texas League. One day in 1940, Metro took off from center field, swerved behind the left fielder, and caught a fly ball in foul territory.

DEEP BREATH

When the Jersey City Giants scored two runs on a bunt that stopped on the third base line in 1940, Montreal Royals third baseman Bert Haas dropped to the ground and blew the ball foul. The runners had to return to their bases.

TECHNICAL DIFFICULTIES

Local radio personality Mike Frankovich caught for the Los Angeles Angels on the last day of the 1940 Pacific Coast League season. Frankovich got ejected, changed uniforms, and caught the final inning for the opposing Oakland Oaks.

A GIANT PITCHER

Seven-foot-tall pitcher Richard Ahrens stood high on the mound for minor league teams in the 1940s. He was considered the tallest pitcher in minor league history until 7-foot-1 Loek van Mil came along in the mid-2000s.

APPLESAUCE

Brockville Pirates pitcher John Grilli threw an apple instead of a baseball during a Class C Canadian-American League game against the Ogdensburg Colts in 1936. The batter swung and smashed the apple. Grilli was ejected.

FALL ASLEEP

Bill Wright, a minor league first baseman in the 1940s, once fell asleep while standing on a 12-foot ladder and fell to the ground.

CAPPED OFF

John Pavoris accidentally threw a ball into his own hat. Pavoris was playing third base for the Class D Kentucky-Illinois-Tennessee League's Fulton Tigers in 1942 when his cap fluttered off while he fielded a grounder with two outs in the ninth inning. His throw went into the cap and took it on a bouncy ride toward first base. Two runners scored and Pavoris was charged with a game-ending error.

PENNY UP

Injured Louisville Colonels catcher Jack Aragon was presented with a washtub full of 50,000 pennies on September 5, 1945. The tub of copper was to help Aragon get back on his feet after he broke his leg the month before.

COLLAPSE

Portland Beavers pitcher Bill Herring sustained minor head injuries in 1943 when Portland's dugout roof crumbled and blocks of cement fell on him.

RABBIT HUNTING

It seems a team named Hoppers would welcome rabbits, but that wasn't true on an August day in 1937. Pitcher Deacon Delmore of the Class D Kentucky-Illinois-Tennessee League's Hopkinsville Hoppers spotted a rabbit darting across left field in the middle of an at bat. He whipped the ball at the bunny and missed.

FIRED UP

Miami Blues catcher Dave Dennis threw down his chest protector after it caught fire during an argument with a Class D Kansas-Oklahoma-Missouri League umpire in 1946. The fire started because a fan tossed a lit cigarette at Dennis.

REPORTS OF MY DEATH ARE GREATLY EXAGGERATED

Durham Bulls fans were pleasantly surprised to see their second baseman Lee Mohr take the field in 1946. United States War Department files previously had said Mohr was killed in World War II.

LASSO

The Class C Gloversville-Johnstown Glovers had an overflow crowd one Sunday in 1946 in Gloversville, New York, and they let excess fans stand on the field behind a rope. Glovers catcher Ben Huffman got tangled chasing a foul pop-up and the rope clamped around his neck and flung him to the ground. His throat hurt so badly that he wasn't able to talk for the rest of the game.

KICKIN' IT

Atlanta Crackers right fielder Babe Ellis was ejected on August 16, 1946, for kicking his glove around the field during a 10-minute argument.

WILD CARD

Amarillo Gold Sox pitcher Steve Lagomarsino had to miss part of the 1947 season after a teammate stabbed him during a poker game.

THE FIX IS IN

In 1947, five players in the Class D Evangeline League were put on baseball's permanently ineligible list for conspiring with gamblers. The players allegedly made intentional mistakes in the field so their teams would lose.

EXHIBITION DEMOLITION

San Antonio Missions left fielder Roy Sievers ran through the outfield fence while chasing a deep fly ball in a 1948 exhibition game against Indianapolis.

HE BLEEDS SCHENECTADY BLUE

Tommy Lasorda is best known as the Hall of Fame manager of the Los Angeles Dodgers, but he was the best minor league pitcher on May 31, 1948. Lasorda pitched all 15 innings, struck out 25 batters, and drove in the game-winning run in the Class C Schenectady Blue Jays' extra-inning win that day.

ASSET MANAGEMENT

Lester Osterman Jr. went from dealing shares to dealing pitches. Osterman, a New York Stock Exchange broker, bought the Class B Colonial League's Port Chester Clippers in 1948 and put himself in to pitch twice.

MIRROR, MIRROR ON THE WALL

In 1949, Class D Easton Yankees pitcher Robert Allison broke his hand when he accidentally pushed his fist through a bathroom mirror while reviewing his pickoff move. The 21-year-old Allison never pitched again after that season.

POW!

The Class D Independence Yankees released infielder Harry Bright in 1947 because he was reading comic books in the dugout during a game.

EIGHT MEN IN

The Texas League's Houston Buffs had only eight players on the field during an inning in 1949 because left fielder Lou Novikoff was in the bathroom. Fans yelled for Novikoff as an opponent placed a hit into unoccupied left field and ran all the way to third base.

BAREHANDED BACKSTOP

Albany Cardinals catcher Hal Smith was feeling antsy when a runner was coming toward him during a 1949 Class D Georgia-Florida League game, and he mistakenly tossed his mitt aside, instead of tossing his mask. He caught the relay throw with his bare hands and tagged the runner for the out.

HALL OF FAME KNOCKOUT

Mickey Mantle is a member of the Baseball Hall of Fame and Bill Hornsby's father, Rogers, is also immortalized in Cooperstown. On August 28, 1949, Mantle was playing for the Class D Independence Yankees and he crushed a ball deep into the outfield against the Carthage Cubs. Bill Hornsby, a Carthage outfielder, lost sight of the baseball and it conked him on the head. Hornsby was knocked unconscious and Mantle rounded the bases.

CLOGGING THE BASES

A drainpipe helped a minor league team win a game. Sometime in the 1940s or 1950s, a center fielder named Frank Lucchesi picked up a batted ball in deep center field, pushed it into an open pipe and pretended the ball was stuck. The umpire ruled it a ground-rule double and made a runner who had scored return to third base. Lucchesi's team won by one run.

TRILINGUAL

Hollywood Stars pitcher Jean-Pierre Roy performed as a singer in nightclubs after games in 1949 and 1950. His show included songs in English, French, and Spanish.

SHE'S A CATCH

Birmingham Barons first baseman Norm Zauchin tumbled into the stands trying to catch a foul ball during a 1950 Southern Association game. He landed on a woman named Janet Mooney, asked her on a date, and they got married two years later.

GO SHORTY

Some people thought Joe Chulla was a batboy. Chulla, the Class C Twin Falls Cowboys' second baseman in 1950, was only 4-foot-5.

FENCED IN

The ball was resting right next to Salt Lake City outfielder Bobby Cherry, but he couldn't reach it. Cherry crashed into the outfield wall in pursuit of Richard Small's fly ball in a Class C Pioneer League game against Billings on May 8, 1951, in Salt Lake City. As he collided with the fence, Cherry's arm went through a hole in the wall and he couldn't wiggle it out. Small rounded the bases for an inside-the-park home run.

A similar episode happened in 1990 when the Triple-A Iowa Cubs' grounds crew had to rescue Indianapolis center fielder Jim Steels during an inning because he collided with the outfield wall and his spikes attached to the fence.

TAILOR-MADE

Sacramento Solons pitchers warmed up before their game in Portland, Oregon, on April 27, 1956, with white polka dots sewn onto their jerseys. They planned on wearing the spotted jerseys during the game to distract Portland's hitters, but the umpire wouldn't let them.

STRONG LEATHER

A stray bullet knocked the glove off Elmira Pioneers center fielder Milt Joffe's hand during a Class A Eastern League game in 1952. Two 17-year-olds were arrested the next day for the shooting. The bullet was stuck in Joffe's glove when he picked it up.

KEEP YOUR MASK ON

When a Pacific Coast League umpire didn't show up to the Portland vs. Sacramento doubleheader on July 21, 1952, Sacramento catcher Vinnie Smith volunteered to umpire all 18 innings. Smith later became a PCL and major league umpire.

SIX OUTS

The Class D Appalachian League's Welch Miners turned triple plays two innings in a row on July 28, 1954. It's believed to be the only time in professional baseball history that a team completed triple plays in consecutive innings.

HE HAD A HOSE

A groundskeeper went from mowing the grass to mowing down hitters on September 8, 1954. The Class B Asheville Tourists had a tired pitching staff, so they signed 54-year-old team groundskeeper, and former professional pitcher, Bud Shaney, who started that day and pitched five shutout innings.

SEATTLE SLEW

The Seattle Rainiers signed softball star Bob Fesler to pitch for them in 1955. Fesler threw dozens of no-hitters in fastpitch softball and he brought his underhand delivery to the Pacific Coast League. But his underhand pitches didn't fool anyone in the PCL. Fesler had a 16.43 ERA through four games and Seattle released him.

THREE-RUN SACRIFICE FLY

Three runs scoring on one sacrifice fly is an infrequent sight, but the rare play happened in the Class D Appalachian League twice in a month's span. On July 7, 1955, Bluefield's Johnny LiPrando whacked a fly ball to center field and Kingsport's Johnny Charles ran it down. But when Charles got tangled in an outfield bush and couldn't throw the ball in, all three Bluefield runners raced around to score.

Just two weeks later, Wytheville's Joe Oxedine socked a deep fly ball to Bristol center fielder Jimmy Flanagan, who slammed into a concrete wall after making the catch. All three Wytheville runners scored as Flanagan lay unconscious on the warning track.

HEADSTRONG

Belmont Chiefs right fielder Eddie Montellanico ran back for a fly ball on June 7, 1961, in a Class D Western Carolina League game and the ball bonked him on the head and flew over the fence for a home run. Montellanico was knocked out briefly but he stayed in the game.

PROTEIN DIET

Austin Braves catcher J. W. Porter ate 24 eggs before a Double-A Texas League game in the mid-1960s.

A NEW HIDDEN-BALL TRICK

Binghamton Triplets left fielder John May hid a ball in his back pocket and brought it with him into the field in the seventh inning on June 25, 1964. When Auburn's Dan Napoleon hit a deep fly ball to left field, May ran back, banged into the wall, pulled the ball out of his pocket, and pretended he made the catch, even though the game ball flew over the fence. The trick worked; the Class A New York-Pennsylvania League umpires believed him and ruled it a catch. When Auburn's manager argued, the umpires got together, brought the kid who caught the home run ball onto the field to question him, and reversed the call 15 minutes later, giving Napoleon a home run.

MORE BALLS IN PLAY

There were two balls in play at the same time in the Fort Worth vs. San Antonio Double-A Texas League game on July 28, 1964. When ball four went to the backstop, the umpire accidentally gave Fort Worth's catcher a new ball. Fort Worth then threw out the batter who walked when he tried to advance to second base because the previous pitch was still live at the backstop. San Antonio argued the situation, the umpires got together, and San Antonio's runner was sent back safely to first base.

KICKBACK

Lou Piniella fought a wall and the wall won. The Triple-A Portland Beavers outfielder took the field between innings of a 1967 game frustrated about his recent at bat. He kicked the outfield fence and the fence toppled on top of him. Portland's relievers rescued the pinned Piniella.

FROG IN YOUR THROAT

Triple-A Indianapolis pitcher Bill Faul bit the head off of a parakeet in 1968 and said he swallowed toads to gain more "hop" on his pitches.

KEEP YOUR EYE ON THE BALL

Columbus Jets catcher Gary Kolb whipped the ball back to pitcher Danny Rivas during a Triple-A game in 1970, but Rivas wasn't looking. The ball clocked Rivas in the head, knocked him out cold, and gave him a gash that required five stitches.

I'M BLUE

Colorful Portland Beavers infielder Frank Peters swung a blue bat, used a blue glove, and wore a blue headband during games in 1971.

ELEVATED FASTBALL

Single-A Cedar Rapids Astros reliever Bob Youse brought new meaning to the phrase "pitching up in the zone" on July 5, 1973. Youse wound up and went through his delivery but the ball slipped out of his hand, flew over the backstop, and onto the roof of the stadium.

MACHO MINOR LEAGUER

Randy Poffo traded grand slams for body slams. Poffo played four seasons in the St. Louis Cardinals' and Cincinnati Reds' organizations in the 1970s as a catcher and outfielder before quitting to become a professional wrestler. You probably know him as "Macho Man" Randy Savage.

BULLPEN BRAINSTORMING

Big League Chew bubble gum was invented in a minor league bullpen. Pitchers Jim Bouton and Rob Nelson were sitting in the Portland Mavericks' bullpen during a 1977 Northwest League game discussing chewing tobacco. Nelson told Bouton his plan for shredded gum packaged in a tobacco-like pouch. Bouton loved the idea and partnered with Nelson on the project. Big League Chew and its cartoonish wrapping is still available today in various flavors.

SCENIC ROUTE

In 1978, Utica Blue Jays infielder Feliberto Corona was traveling from the Dominican Republic to Utica, New York, to join his team. He left the New York City airport during his layover, thinking he was in Utica, and asked a cab driver to take him to Utica's ballpark. The fare for the 240-mile cab ride was $393.

MONEYBALL

High-A Lynchburg Mets outfielder Billy Beane acted as if he caught a ball that actually bounced past him in 1981. The umpires believed Beane's charade and called Durham's batter out.

HAVE WE MET BEFORE?

Pitcher Robin Fuson beaned Darryl Strawberry in a 1981 fall instructional league game. Fuson became an assistant district attorney in Florida and prosecuted Strawberry in a drug case two decades later.

GOING OUT WITH A BANG

Triple-A Portland Beavers pitcher Mark Lee was informed before the game on August 17, 1982, that he would be released the following day. The Beavers needed relievers that night and Lee was called on to pitch. He decided to leave baseball on his own terms, and after striking out a Vancouver batter for the second out of the ninth inning, he tossed away the ball, threw off his cap, ripped off his jersey, ran into the dugout, and kept on running into retirement.

HANDS FREE

A team turned a triple play without touching the ball in 1986. A group of Houston Astros minor leaguers were playing Chicago White Sox minor leaguers in an extended spring training game in Sarasota, Florida. The White Sox team had runners at first and second with no outs. Both runners took off on a hit-and-run and the batter hit a pop-up. The infield fly rule was called for the first out, the runner from first passed the runner on second for the second out, and the pop-up landed on the remaining runner for the third out.

DOWN IN FLAMES

Triple-A Phoenix Firebirds pitcher Ed Lynch allowed 15 earned runs on May 7, 1988, and retired on the spot. Lynch's disastrous outing came at Spurgeon Field in Colorado Springs, Colorado, where small dimensions, 70 mph winds, and the high elevation led to a 33-12 score that day. After Lynch surrendered a fifth home run, he walked off the field, packed his belongings, and hung up his spikes.

BLING

Triple-A Indianapolis pitcher Yorkis Perez suffered a 24-karat injury in 1990 when his thick gold chain bounced out of his jersey and popped him in the eye. Perez went on the injured list and had to wear sunglasses in the dugout, even during night games.

PERMISSION SLIP

The Pioneer League's Pocatello Posse acquired a toddler in 1993. Four-year-old Kyle Carnaroli won a contest to join the team and play right field in a game. Minor League Baseball's office heard about the prize and nixed it because Carnaroli could've gotten hurt.

GOOD COACHING

There weren't any meetings with the pitching coach during Larry Carter's no-hitter for the independent Texas-Louisiana League's Tyler Wildcatters on June 21, 1994, because Carter was the pitching coach. The Wildcatters had signed/hired the former major leaguer to be a player/coach.

IDENTICAL

Mark Mimbs and his identical twin brother, Mike, had the same results on the same night. On May 6, 1995, Mark pitched six scoreless innings for Triple-A Albuquerque, allowing just one Phoenix hit. His brother Mike pitched six scoreless innings for Philadelphia, allowing just one Atlanta hit. The two also had the same number of walks, strikeouts, and hit batters.

SINGING THE BLUES

In 1996, the independent Big South League's Meridian Brakemen traded first baseman Andre Keene to the Greenville Bluesmen for $750 and a Muddy Waters blues album.

LEFTY-RIGHTY MATCHUP

Ambidextrous Johnstown Steal pitcher Jamie Irving confused an independent Frontier League umpire one night in the late 1990s. Irving finished the fifth inning throwing left-handed and when he began the sixth inning throwing right-handed, the umpire pulled out his lineup card, faced the press box, and signaled that a new pitcher had entered the game.

IT'S A BOY!

The Double-A Jackson Generals held a baby shower for rehabbing Houston Astros pitcher Billy Wagner on August 2, 1998. Fans who brought a gift were admitted free and invited to present the gift to Wagner on the field before the game. Wagner's son was born a few days earlier.

OZZIE SMITH'S MOVE

Triple-A Memphis Redbirds infielder and fan favorite Stubby Clapp occasionally did backflips when taking the field in the early 2000s.

OVERNIGHT PARKING ALLOWED

Pitcher Rod Beck made millions of dollars in his MLB career, but when he was back in the minors as a 34-year-old with Triple-A Iowa in 2003, he lived in his RV in the stadium parking lot. Fans stopped by the RV to hang out with Beck after games.

THE MOST MAGICAL PLACE ON EARTH

Double-A Mobile BayBears outfielder Alex Fernandez received a lifetime ban from Disney World because of an incident on July 24, 2002. The BayBears were playing a road game against the Orlando Rays, whose ballpark was inside Disney World's property, and Fernandez pushed down a Rays' mascot. The woman inside the mascot costume said she sustained a concussion, Disney security investigated, and Fernandez was told in writing to never come back.

BROCKTON'S BAD NEWS

The independent Brockton Rox reunited the pitcher and catcher from *The Bad News Bears* in 2005, three decades after the hit movie. Actors Rudi Stein and Mike Engleberg signed one-day contracts with the team and became the starting battery against Elmira in Brockton, Massachusetts, on August 1, 2005.

PITCH COUNT

The first pitch came at 10:44 a.m. for the High-A Brevard County Manatees' night game on August 27, 2005. It was the first of 4,218 first pitches to set a world record. The Manatees invited everyone in their community to come by the stadium throughout the day and throw out a ceremonial first pitch. Local radio stations urged highway drivers to take a detour, throw out a first pitch, and then continue on their travels. The final first pitch came eight hours after the first one.

PITCH MAN

Nigel Thatch, the actor who played a cocky athlete named Leon in 2005 Budweiser commercials, pitched for the independent Schaumburg Flyers that year until he was traded to the Fullerton Flyers for 60 cases of Budweiser.

YOU'VE PROBABLY SEEN THE VIDEO

Fifteen years after Triple-A Vancouver's Rodney McCray ran through the outfield fence at Portland, Oregon's Civic Stadium, the Portland Beavers brought McCray back in 2006, named the site of his infamous wreckage "McCray Alley," and gave out Rodney McCray bobblefence dolls.

BUTTON UP

Three Double-A Tennessee Smokies combined to bring a no-hitter into the eighth inning on September 3, 2006, when Mobile's Colt Morton hit a ground ball to third base. Third baseman Agustin Murillo juggled the ball and couldn't find it anywhere after it sprung out of his glove. Murillo finally realized the baseball had slipped into his shirt. It was scored as a single, ending the no-hit bid.

In 1953, a left fielder stuffed a ball under his jersey on purpose during a Class D game in Pauls Valley, Oklahoma. He claimed the ball bounced through a hole in the outfield fence, which would've given the batter only a double, but the suspicious umpire frisked him, found the ball, and gave the batter a home run.

TWO-TIME CY YOUNG AWARD WINNER

Tim Lincecum pitched in a home game for the Triple-A Fresno Grizzlies on April 23, 2007, the same day a bulldog got loose from the clubhouse and ran onto the infield.

BATHROOM DELAY

Mobile BayBears reliever Matt Elliott got stuck in the dugout bathroom during a Double-A game in Montgomery, Alabama, on June 23, 2007. Elliott allowed the game-tying run in the eighth inning, slammed the bathroom door in frustration after the inning, and broke the door's locking mechanism.

He was trapped in the bathroom for 47 minutes and Mobile had to bring in a new pitcher for the ninth inning. Elliott was eventually rescued by the Montgomery Fire Department.

ULNAR COLLATERAL LIGAMENT RECONSTRUCTION

Tommy John surgery is named after former MLB pitcher Tommy John, who became the first pitcher to have the elbow procedure in 1974. When John managed the independent Atlantic League's Bridgeport Bluefish in 2008, the team had a Tommy John bobble arm giveaway. The bobble arm doll was like a bobblehead but with a moving arm.

SENIOR SPACEMAN

Twenty-five miles and 35 years away from pitching in the 1975 World Series at Boston's Fenway Park, Bill "Spaceman" Lee set the record for oldest pitcher to win a professional game. The independent Brockton Rox signed Lee to a one-day contract on September 5, 2010, and the 63-year-old beat the Worcester Tornadoes, who scored just two runs against Lee in his five innings.

CALL OF DUTY

Speaking of aging hurlers, former Negro Leagues star Ted "Double Duty" Radcliffe pitched in a game at age 96 for the independent Northern League's Schaumburg Flyers on June 19, 1999. He threw one pitch, became the oldest professional pitcher in history, and walked off the mound to a standing ovation.

LAST MAN STANDING

A contest within a contest evolved on August 25, 2012, in the High-A California League. Relievers for both Lake Elsinore and Lancaster stood for the national anthem but didn't sit down. It was a test of endurance. As the innings unfolded, individual pitchers on both sides occasionally bowed out and plopped down. Each bullpen still had one pitcher standing strong when the actual game ended. The two pitchers negotiated a truce, settled on a tie, and sat down, four hours after the national anthem ended.

The last-man-standing contests became a trend and umpires weren't happy about it. Triple-A Fresno pitcher Jose Veras was ejected for standing on the field too long after the national anthem on June 27, 2015, in Reno, Nevada.

GREAT-GRANDMA'S GRAB

Anne Kenyon was 91 years old when she caught a foul ball barehanded at a High-A San Jose Giants game on June 15, 2012. The team had her come back three weeks later to throw out a ceremonial first pitch. Kenyon had 15 great-grandchildren at the time.

SKUNKED

Frederick Keys pitcher Miguel Chalas picked up a live skunk with his glove during a 2013 High-A game in Lynchburg, Virginia. Chalas thought it was a cat. He wasn't familiar with skunks because there aren't any native to the Dominican Republic, his home country.

BAD DAY

Nick Greenwood was the losing pitcher for two teams on the same day. On June 10, 2013, Triple-A Memphis lost the completion of a game suspended two months earlier and Greenwood was the pitcher of record. In the two months between the Memphis game starting and ending, Greenwood was demoted to Double-A Springfield, where he also lost their game on June 10.

WALL NINJA

In 2013, Single-A Beloit Snappers reliever Dakota Bacus occasionally dressed in all white, covertly walked on the warning track, and stood in front of a white wall advertisement, in fair territory, while the game was going on. He was never caught by an umpire.

18 DAYS, 630 MILES, 0 HITS

The Triple-A Rochester Red Wings pitched a no-hitter using two pitchers in multiple ballparks in multiple states. Trevor May threw three hitless innings in Durham, North Carolina, on July 24, 2014, before the game was halted by rain. The game continued in Rochester, New York, on August 11 and May's teammate Logan Darnell tossed six innings to finalize the no-hitter. It's the only no-hitter in professional baseball history to start in one stadium and finish in another.

ZIPPED THROUGH THE LINEUP

Jake Thompson pitched six innings with his fly down on August 26, 2014. The Double-A Frisco righty busted his zipper while warming up before the game and Frisco was on the road in Corpus Christi, Texas, so Thompson didn't have a backup pair of pants.

GUT CHECK

Triple-A Pawtucket catcher Humberto Quintero tried to catch a Durham runner stealing third on May 2, 2015, but his throw never arrived. He accidentally fired the ball into Durham right-handed batter Luke Maile's stomach. Maile fell over in pain.

LOST IN TRANSLATION

Chien-Ming Wang pranked his Triple-A Tacoma Rainiers coaches on the final day of the 2015 season by filling out the official pitchers' chart in traditional Chinese, his native language.

THE INDIANA TWINS

David and Ryan Ledbetter are twin brothers from Indianapolis who pitched in the Texas Rangers' minor league system together from 2013–2016. They occasionally pitched for the same Rangers affiliate on the same day.

DOWNWARD DOG

On April 19, 2016, a wild throw from Triple-A Tacoma shortstop Chris Taylor in El Paso, Texas, flew into the first base dugout and knocked down Chico, the chihuahua mascot for the El Paso Chihuahuas. The mascot showed up the next day with one of his fuzzy arms in a sling.

HOW?

The Single-A South Atlantic League's Charleston RiverDogs struck out five Augusta batters in one inning on April 21, 2016. Two of the strikeout victims reached first base on a third strike wild pitch, which doesn't count as an out but does count as a strikeout for a pitcher's stats.

GROUNDS-BREAKING

On July 8, 2016, Single-A Delmarva Shorebirds employees couldn't get the tarp on the field when a sudden storm arrived in the bottom of the fifth inning with the Shorebirds ahead 5-0. Delmarva starter Ofelky Peralta hadn't allowed any hits in his five innings and he entered the South Atlantic League record book for his rain-shortened no-hitter.

BUMPER TO BUMPER

San Francisco Giants infielder Ehire Adrianza was in Triple-A Sacramento's lineup for an injury rehab appearance on July 22, 2016, but was removed because he got stuck in traffic driving from San Francisco to Sacramento.

PICKING UP THE TAB

When well-paid major leaguers join minor league teams on injury rehab assignments, they often pay for a catered meal in the clubhouse as a gift to their minor league teammates. On June 22, 2016, San Francisco Giants pitcher Sergio Romo paid for a taco truck to park in the players' parking lot and feed his Triple-A Sacramento River Cats teammates after his rehab game in Sacramento, California.

SHOCKING CALL

In the early 1990s at Huntsville, Alabama's Joe Davis Stadium, a Double-A pitcher flinched because of a close lightning bolt and was called for a balk.

SUBTRACTION

Triple-A Las Vegas reliever David Roseboom went from number 12 to number 2 during an inning on April 7, 2017. Roseboom wound up, and as he delivered a pitch, the numeral 1 popped off the back of his jersey and fluttered to the ground. He picked up the single digit, walked it off the field, returned to the mound, and finished the inning as number 2.

LOW PITCH

Triple-A Rochester Red Wings pitcher John Curtiss played guitar and sang the national anthem before Rochester's home game on September 2, 2018.

BUT WE HAVEN'T EVEN STARTED YET!

Triple-A Salt Lake Bees reliever Justin Miller was ejected before his team's home game on April 30, 2017, after a shouting match with the first base umpire about the location of his chair in the on-field bullpen.

GUSTY

Six days later, on the same day the National Weather Service issued a high wind warning for Salt Lake City, Bees pitcher Troy Scribner was pushed off the mound by strong wind while in the set position. He was charged with a balk, moving an Omaha runner from second to third.

OLDEST TRICK IN THE BOOK

Triple-A Rochester Red Wings third baseman Jermaine Curtis pulled off a successful hidden ball trick on April 18, 2018. Charlotte's Kevan Smith was talking to his third base coach and began walking into his lead. Curtis still had the ball and he lunged over and tagged Smith for the out.

BROTHERHOOD

Members of the Triple-A Colorado Springs Sky Sox bullpen were yelling at the first base umpire late in a lopsided home game against Nashville on May 3, 2018. The umpire had enough, turned around, and ejected someone, but nobody was sure who got tossed, so the relievers stood up in unison and walked off the field together.

RULE 6.09

The Single-A Wisconsin Timber Rattlers trailed by two runs with two outs and two strikes in the bottom of the ninth inning on August 10, 2018. A third strike on a pitch in the dirt looked like it would end the game but Burlington catcher Keinner Pina's throw to first base went down the right field line and three Wisconsin runners scored to win the game.

BALK-OFF WIN

The final pitch of the 2018 Northwest League season wasn't a pitch at all. The Eugene Emeralds' championship-winning run scored when Spokane Indians pitcher Emmanuel Clase stumbled and balked with a runner at third.

AMBIDEXTROUS HURLER

Pat Venditte last pitched in the minors in 2019 with Triple-A Sacramento. When he faced switch hitters, the "Venditte Rule" stated he had to commit his glove to one hand before an at bat, which showed the batter which hand he intended to pitch with. The switch hitter then decided which side of the plate to hit from. The Professional Baseball Umpires Corporation created the rule because the switch pitcher vs. switch hitter matchups were causing confusion when Venditte pitched. One of Venditte's former teams, the Staten Island Yankees, gave out "Pat Venditte Bobblearms" figures to 2,500 fans on August 19, 2016.

BRAGGING RIGHTS

The Philadelphia Phillies had two affiliates in the Gulf Coast League in 2019, and on June 26 of that year, GCL Phillies West threw a combined no-hitter against GCL Phillies East.

DOUBLEHEADER NO-HITTER

Two years earlier, also in the Gulf Coast League, the Washington Nationals' affiliate threw two no-hitters against the Miami Marlins' affiliate on July 23, 2017.

STRESS-FREE SAVE

The Dominican Summer League Yankees smoked the Dominican Summer League Twins 38-2 on July 3, 2019. Yankees reliever Luis Velasquez was given a save in the 36-run rout because he pitched the final four innings.

GOOD HANDS

Infielder Derek Dietrich has played in the minor leagues for parts or all of every season since 2010 and he's also an expert juggler who used to work for a circus. Dietrich has occasionally entertained minor league fans with pregame juggling shows involving bowling pins, flaming torches, and knives.

MORE DOMINICAN SUMMER LEAGUE CHAOS

The DSL Mariners beat one of the Yankees' DSL clubs 22-21 on July 22, 2021, in a 10-inning game that took six hours and 35 minutes to complete.

TRADED FOR HIMSELF

Relief pitcher Myles Smith was traded from the independent Milwaukee Milkmen to the independent Long Island Ducks for a player to be named later in September 2019. One month later, Smith was sent from the Ducks back to the Milkmen as the player to be named later to complete the trade.

THROW STRIKES!

The Double-A Birmingham Barons walked 13 Biloxi batters in one inning in Birmingham, Alabama, on May 6, 2021.

USED EQUIPMENT

The Single-A Lynchburg Hillcats were without a first baseman's mitt for their road game against the Carolina Mudcats on July 6, 2021, so Mudcats first baseman Ashton McGee left his mitt on first base at the end of each half inning for the Hillcats to use.

GETTING AROUND

Later that season, Mudcats utility man Noah Campbell played all nine positions and got the save in Carolina's 5-2 win over the Fayetteville Woodpeckers on September 19, 2021.

HONEYMOONERS

Single-A Daytona Tortugas outfielder Leo Seminati married his wife, Carissa, on the field between innings of Daytona's game on September 3, 2021.

Maybe the Seminatis could double-date with Daytona's married turtle mascots, Shelldon and Shelly.

OH HENRY!

The San Diego Padres have a minor league pitcher named Henry Henry.

MANAGERS & EXECUTIVES

ALL-IN

Scranton manager Dan O'Leary bet his team's monthly payroll on one of their Pennsylvania State Association games in 1886 and he told his players about it as motivation. They went to bat inspired, scored nine runs in the first inning, won 20-6, and celebrated all night at a saloon with their extra money.

PROTESTERS

It's rare to see a manager protest a game and it's even rarer to see both managers protest the same game. Duluth's William Lucas and his Oshkosh counterpart both filed protests after playing each other on June 14, 1886, in Oshkosh, Wisconsin, and both gave "incompetent umpiring" as the reason.

LETTERMAN

The Denison-Sherman Twins had two owners in 1896, one based in Denison, Texas, and the other in Sherman, Texas. When manager Pete Weckbecker had a contract dispute with the Sherman owner, he ripped the S off the front of his jersey, leaving only a D.

SAVANNAH SCAM

Savannah players had their manager A.C. Cooper arrested on May 16, 1898, for pocketing the club's payment for a road game in Mobile, Alabama. He was supposed to split the cash among his players. Cooper had the last laugh though. He kept the players' train tickets too, so they were stranded in Mobile.

WHISTLE WHILE YOU WORK

Lew Whistler managed two New York minor league teams in 1899; one fired him and the other had him arrested. Whistler's Syracuse Stars club didn't win many games, so he was let go. He then joined the Schenectady Electricians as a player/manager, before getting arrested for misappropriating the team's funds.

I WANT MY MONEY BACK

Houston Buffaloes management stopped its team's Texas Association game on May 3, 1899, and refunded fans' money because of their players' "indifferent play."

FROZEN FISH

Early 1900s Sioux City Packers manager Ducky Holmes used to fish foul balls out of the nearby Missouri River, put the wet baseballs in a freezer, and have his pitchers use them in the next day's game. Opposing batters couldn't hit the frozen balls forcefully.

DISGUISES

Newark Indians manager Harry Smith got ejected from a game in 1912, dressed up like a "mad Russian," and sat in the stands while yelling orders to his team in a fake accent.

In 1914, Venice Tigers manager Hap Hogan got thrown out of a game, put on a Panama hat and frock coat over his uniform, and gave signs from the right field stands.

CLEANING HOUSE

New Orleans Pelicans manager/owner Abner Powell was frustrated by his team's last place results in July 1901, so he traveled to North Carolina, signed an entire team from a lower-level league, released his previous squad, and suggested they sit in the stands to "watch a real team." The new-look Pelicans won 80 percent of their games down the stretch.

DREDLY FORCE

Class D Texarkana's Dred Cavender wasn't a players' manager. When his shortstop committed two errors in a 1902 game, Cavender chased the player and shot at him. The infielder scurried to the outfield wall and hopped over the fence, dodging two bullets along the way.

STONED

The Minneapolis Millers were playing a game in Toledo, Ohio, in 1903 when a 10-year-old fan was pelting them with stones. Minneapolis manager George Yeager punched the young fan and was arrested and charged with assault.

DIRTY LAUNDRY

Class A Louisville Colonels president George Tebeau was outraged at a decision made by umpire George Bausewine during a 1904 game and was shouting at Bausewine from the stands. The umpire ignored the executive, so Tebeau broke into Bausewine's dressing room, took his clothes out of the locker, left the stadium, and threw the umpire's clothes all over the road. Tebeau was suspended 10 days by the American Association.

TWO-STEP

Herman Long was 39 years old with a weakening arm when he played for the Class A Des Moines Underwriters in 1905 and opposing batters reached base repeatedly after hitting ground balls to him, so Underwriters owner Mike Cantillon moved first base from 90 feet to 92 feet from home plate so Long could throw out more runners.

B-SQUAD

Class B Worcester Busters manager Jesse Burkett sent a mishmash of backup players and fill-ins to go lose a road game in Lowell, Massachusetts, on June 13, 1907, while Burkett's regulars stayed in Worcester to play a major league exhibition against the St. Louis Browns. The exhibition made Burkett more money than the regular season road game would have.

HOW TIMES HAVE CHANGED

Class B Seattle manager Dan Dugdale was ejected on May 19, 1908, because he ordered his pitcher to throw a "slow ball" to an Aberdeen hitter. He was also fined $5.

LET'S TURN THREE

Class D Portsmouth Cobblers manager Pete Childs angrily watched his pitcher load the bases with no outs on June 21, 1910. He stormed to the mound, grabbed the baseball, and inserted himself as pitcher. Childs hadn't pitched professionally in 13 years, yet he ended the rally on his first pitch when Marion's batter hit into a triple play.

SPARE CHANGE

An infant acted like a baby in 1917. Class D La Crosse Infants manager Jay Andrews paid an ejection fine by dumping a sack of pennies on the umpire's feet before the next day's Central Association game.

HAIL TO THE CHIEF

Warren Harding was president of the United States from 1921–1923. A decade earlier, he was part-owner of the Class D Marion Diggers in Ohio. Harding was the first U. S. president to have owned part of a professional baseball club.

QUALITY CONTROL

After the Austin Senators won only 31 of their 145 games in 1914, their owner was punished by the Texas League for "gross mismanagement."

INELIGIBLE RECEIVER

When a wild throw went into the first base dugout in 1915 in St. Paul, Minnesota, St. Paul Saints manager Mike Kelley picked up the ball and threw it to his catcher, who tagged out a Columbus Senators runner. The umpire missed that it was the manager who threw the ball and the out call stood.

GET READY

In 1917, Class B Eastern League president Dan O'Neil mandated that pitchers get only three warm-up tosses between innings. His new rule was enacted to quicken the pace of play.

WAKE-UP CALL

Minneapolis Millers manager Joe Cantillon fell asleep in the dugout during a game one day in 1917 or 1918. Minneapolis infielder Carl Sawyer filled a bucket with cold water and dumped it on his sleeping manager, who woke up confused and asking if it was raining.

TRANSFER OF POWER

Class D Enid Harvesters manager Barney Childs released wealthy first baseman Dud Branom during a Western Association game in 1920 and Branom wanted payback. He left the clubhouse, went to the bank in downtown Enid, Oklahoma, bought the ballpark and team, returned to the field, fired Childs, and put himself in charge for the rest of the season.

DRUNK DEAL

Hall of Fame executive Branch Rickey bought a 50 percent stake in the Syracuse Stars franchise from inebriated Stars owner Ernest Landgraf at a 1921 baseball convention.

LIVES AND DIES WITH HIS TEAM

Class A Omaha Buffaloes general manager Mickey Finn had heart problems in 1922, so doctors made him take two weeks off of work. The day he returned to the ballpark, a fourth inning rally by visiting Tulsa made Finn collapse in the stands and die of a heart attack.

GROUNDED

Two years later, Buffaloes owner Barney Burch tried to trade two players for an airplane. He offered catchers Roy Luebbe and Fred Wilder to the Class A St. Joseph Saints in exchange for the Saints' owner's plane. The deal didn't get off the runway.

MONOPOLY

The St. Louis Cardinals went on a spending spree in the 1920s and bought dozens of minor league clubs to give themselves a vast pool of talent. At one point, every team in the Class D Nebraska State League was owned by the Cardinals.

TOO EARLY?

When the Baltimore Orioles lost the Junior World Series in 1923, manager Jack Dunn went on a tirade and released one of his pitchers and one of his catchers for warming up too early.

POWER STRUGGLE

Two men claimed to be Pacific Coast League president in November 1923. Newspaper writer Harry Williams got more votes than incumbent William McCarthy, but McCarthy refused to concede and held his own separate league meetings. One month later, the National Arbitration Board named Williams president.

TWO-WAY? NO WAY!

Tulsa Oilers manager Jack Lelivelt was fined $100 by the Class A Western League in 1924 for using a position player as a pitcher.

DUCK NEST

When Dayton Ducks manager Ducky Holmes got thrown out of games in the 1930s, he sometimes walked across the street, climbed onto a house's roof that overlooked the field, and flashed signals to his players from that elevated view.

STOPLIGHT

Fresco Thompson, a minor league manager in the 1930s and 1940s, once brought a two-way, multi-colored flashlight to the third-base coaches box during a Southern Association game. He turned on a green light to send runners home and a red light to hold them at third.

DEALT FOR DOUGHNUTS

The Class A San Antonio Indians traded infielder Len Dondero to the Dallas Steers for a dozen doughnuts in 1930. MLB commissioner Kenesaw Mountain Landis later disallowed the sweet deal.

SHOWTIME

The Pacific Coast League's Hollywood Stars had 11 movie stars as partial owners in the 1940s, including Bing Crosby and George Burns. The ballclub's slogan was "the Hollywood Stars baseball team, owned by the Hollywood stars."

HOT STOVE

A player was traded for a turkey in 1931. Class A Chatta-nooga Lookouts owner Joe Engel sent shortstop Johnny Jones to Charlotte and received a turkey in return. Engel explained "the turkey was having a better year," before serving his new acquisition at a banquet.

SPEAKING OF TURKEY

There was a turkey walking around on the warning track during the Triple-A Buffalo Bisons' home game on April 6, 2022.

HANGOVER

Manager Nick Williams led San Francisco to the 1931 Pacific Coast League championship but was fired three days later for excessive drinking.

FRUITY

In 1933, the San Francisco Seals acquired Memphis Chicks first baseman Jack Fenton in exchange for a case of prunes.

LENIENT

Oakland manager Ray Brubaker and Sacramento manager Earl McNeely got into a fistfight during a Pacific Coast League game on May 4, 1933. Even though Brubaker was bleeding after the scuffle, nobody was ejected.

CONTRAT SIGNE

The National Association of Professional Baseball Leagues was surprised to receive a contract written in French on February 13, 1935. When French-Canadian outfielder Gus Dugas came to terms with the Montreal Royals, the team and player both agreed the contract should be written in their preferred language.

SNOW BOWL

Class D Snow Hill Billies manager Peahead Walker left his baseball seasons early in the late 1930s to report for his other job, head football coach at Wake Forest University.

LIBERATED

MLB commissioner Kenesaw Mountain Landis made 91 minor leaguers in the Detroit Tigers' organization free agents on January 14, 1940, to penalize the Tigers for falsifying documents about their affiliates and their minor league players.

FLEXIBLE FENCES

The 1940s Milwaukee Brewers of the American Association varied the height of their outfield walls depending on the opponent. Milwaukee's Borchert Field was squeezed within a tight set of streets, placing the foul poles only 267 feet from home plate. Owner Bill Veeck purchased massive, portable fences and installed them for games against top-hitting teams. When Veeck felt the Brewers were the better hitting team, the movable fences stayed backstage.

SPLISH-SPLASH FLIP-FLOP

The Class D Salisbury Cardinals cancelled a game in 1941 after three inches of rainwater filled the infield. Salisbury's owner arrived after a 14-hour drive and wanted to see a ballgame, so the team changed its mind and announced the game was back on. Only 25 fans watched the players slosh through the water.

HOW'D THEY MANAGE THAT?

The 1943 Southern League All-Star Game skills competition included a wheelbarrow race between league managers. The skippers were blindfolded before running to second base while pushing wheelbarrows.

A BASEBALL GIANT

Pro football Hall of Famer Ken Strong was president of the Class B Colonial League in 1947 while he was an active football player for the New York Giants.

BOOM GOES THE DYNAMITE

On September 11, 1948, Class A Fort Wayne Generals manager Boom Boom Beck ran up to the home plate umpire during an argument, ripped off the ump's mask, and threw it 75 feet away. Beck was suspended indefinitely and fined $100.

OTHER DUTIES AS ASSIGNED

Ray "Little Buffalo" Perry was the Class D Redding Browns' president/general manager/bus driver/athletic trainer/infielder in 1948. He won the Far West League batting title that year and also served as the league's vice president.

MAKING A SPLASH

One day in the late 1940s, Durham Bulls manager Willie Duke dumped a bucket of water on home plate to protest a call. He was ejected.

ROCKY RELATIONSHIP

Rocky Mount Leafs president Frank Walker was suspended indefinitely by the Class D Coastal Plain League on June 25, 1949, for punching an umpire after a game.

CAUGHT WITH A CAMERA

Great Falls Electrics general manager Nick Mariana videotaped a mysterious saucer flying above his ballpark in Great Falls, Montana, on August 15, 1950. It's considered one of the earliest UFO videos and experts refer to the sighting as "The Mariana Incident."

CHOKEHOLD

Miami Sun Sox manager Pepper Martin was suspended and fined $100 on September 1, 1949, for choking a Class B Florida International League umpire.

OFF-ROADING

A manager drove his car on the field in 1950. Class B Terre Haute Phillies skipper Danny Carnevale was disappointed with the condition of the infield dirt at Terre Haute, Indiana's Memorial Stadium, so he took matters into his own wheels. Carnevale attached a harrow to the back of his sedan, had a player sit on it to weigh it down, and drove around, grooming the infield.

STOGIES

In 1951, longtime team owner Bill Veeck sold his stake in the Oklahoma City Indians to Jimmie Humphries for a box of cigars.

SURVEY SAYS

The National Association of Professional Baseball Leagues polled all minor league team owners in 1951 and asked what their day jobs were. The answers included 12 florists, 18 morticians, and 18 housewives.

SUPER SOAKER

Double-A Birmingham Barons manager Jimmy Piersall got ejected from a hot afternoon home game in 1952, climbed onto the ballpark's roof with a water pistol, and sprayed the fans behind home plate.

BUNT HIM OVER . . . OVER.

Frank Lucchesi managed a game via walkie-talkie. Lucchesi, the Class C Pine Bluff Judges' manager from 1953–1954, was serving a suspension and was banned from the ballpark, so he sat in a van behind the outfield wall, peered into the field, and transmitted his orders from a walkie-talkie to someone in Pine Bluff's dugout.

PASS THE PAIL

Lucchesi got salty then sandy one night in the 1960s. He got ejected from a game and refused to leave the field, sitting on home plate making sand castles until security escorted him to the clubhouse.

NOSEBLEED SEATS

Okay, one more Lucchesi managing story. When he was leading the Triple-A Arkansas Travelers in 1963, he got thrown out of a game, left the ballpark, walked down the street, climbed a water tower, and watched the game from 150 feet above the field.

DRIED OIL

In January 1954, baseball executives in Arkansas and Texas formed a six-team circuit and named it the Oil States League. The league folded two weeks later, without ever playing a game.

PINCH HIT PARADE

Bobby Bragan appeared indecisive on May 1, 1955. The Hollywood Stars' manager sent up eight straight pinch hitters for the same batter in a game against Los Angeles. Fans howled and sportswriters grumbled at the unprofessionalism of dispatching batter after batter, with none of them actually completing the at bat. League president Claire Goodwin fined Bragan $50 for his pinch hitter procession.

WHO CARES?

The Vancouver Mounties didn't take the last game of the 1956 season seriously. Fifty-nine-year-old manager Lefty O'Doul put himself and 51-year-old coach Eddie Taylor in as pinch hitters, and both of them got hits!

CALL THE ROOFER

In 1957, Fitzgerald Orioles manager Earl Weaver got into a cross-field shouting match with Waycross player Bill McKeon during a Class D Georgia-Florida League game. Weaver rumbled across the field and started swinging at the entire Waycross team. One hulking player lifted the diminutive Weaver and pushed his head through the dugout roof.

PROVING HIS POINT

Los Angeles Angels manager Clay Bryant felt a 1957 game should be postponed because of rain, but umpire Mel Steiner disagreed and started the game on time. Bryant put on a raincoat and a rain hat in the first inning and walked to the mound to talk to his pitcher.

ALL ABOARD

The Class A Western League's Topeka Hawks were in first place on July 13, 1957, when their manager Red Smith resigned to take a job with the Texas & Pacific Railroad.

BELLHOP BULLETS

Ardmore Cardinals manager J. C. Dunn survived after being shot in the dugout during a Class D game in Ponca City, Oklahoma, on August 8, 1957. The shooter was hotel porter James Johnson, who had an argument with multiple members of the Cardinals earlier in the day.

SHOTS FIRED

In 1960, Class B Wilson Tobs manager and third base coach Jack McKeon was growing tired of base runner Juan Vistuer ignoring his stop signs. McKeon bought a starter pistol, loaded it with blanks, and brought it to the third base coaches box one night in Greensboro, North Carolina. When Vistuer again ran past a stop sign, McKeon fired a few shots. Vistuer was convinced the gunshots were real, so he fell to the ground to take cover and then retreated to third base.

HEADSTANDS

El Paso Sun Kings manager Rocky Bridges stood on his head in the third base coaches box while giving signs during a Double-A Texas League game in 1967. Sun Kings batter Ethan Blackaby stepped outside the box and stood on his head to receive the signs.

SIGNAL

In 1962, Jack McKeon was managing the Triple-A Vancouver Mounties and he had his pitchers stick a radio receiver in their jersey pocket. McKeon then spoke into a small microphone from the bench, dispensing in-game instructions. McKeon received interference from rival managers, who wondered if the dugout device was legal, but the National Association of Professional Baseball Leagues said it was legal at the time.

THE WEATHERMAN

In the 1960s, Ken Nicolson was president of the Class A Duluth-Superior Dukes and chief meteorologist of the Duluth, Minnesota, weather bureau. A bad day at one job led to a bad night at the other in August 1963. Nicolson predicted a drought, so his groundskeeper soaked the field. His forecast was wrong, it started pouring, and the game was cancelled.

CONTEMPT

Reno Silver Sox manager Tom Saffell was fined $250 and suspended 30 days by the Class A California League for refusing to bring his lineup card to home plate before the game on May 20, 1964. Saffell refused because he was mad at the umpire.

EX-EXPO EJECTED

Single-A Kane County Cougars manager Mark Grudzielanek did bring out his lineup card before a game in Burlington, Iowa, on April 29, 2015, but was tossed during the plate meeting for something he said.

FIRESIDE CHAT

The Albuquerque Dodgers' radio broadcaster had laryngitis on April 18, 1965, so Double-A Texas League president Hugh Finnerty filled in on play-by-play.

USHERING IN A NEW ERA

The Class A Bakersfield Dodgers fired their GM in 1969 and hired a stadium usher to replace him.

HOBBLING HALL OF FAMER

When Warren Spahn managed the Triple-A Tulsa Oilers in 1970, he coached third base with a crutch under each arm because he was recovering from knee surgery.

THE THREE MUSKETEERS

The Mexico City Reds hired three managers for the 1971 season. One worked home games and the other two split duties on the road.

FORE!

Double-A Asheville Orioles manager Cal Ripken Sr. wanted his ballplayers focused on baseball, so he wasn't happy when one of his pitchers brought golf clubs on a 1972 road trip. Ripken seized the clubs, dumped out the golf balls, and whacked them one by one into the woods behind the stadium.

SOUR LEMON

Sacramento Solons manager Bob Lemon switched his team's dugout from the first base side to the third base side during the 1974 season to get away from a fan who constantly heckled him from the first base stands.

CASTAWAYS

The owner of the Class A Seguin Toros wouldn't pay for hotel rooms for a road trip to Corpus Christi, Texas, in 1976, demanding that the team ride a bus back two hours after each game of the series. The players refused the round-trip bus rides and slept on a Corpus Christi beach instead.

DESIGNATED DRIVER

For one night in 1980, Single-A Stockton Ports manager Tony Muser added "Bus Driver" to his job description. Muser was chatting with the team bus driver after a series-ending game in Bakersfield, California, and smelled alcohol on the driver's breath. When Muser confronted him, the driver admitted to drinking during the game. Muser had only one choice–steer the team home himself. He grabbed a map for the four-hour trip and rumbled the bus safely into Stockton while the soon-to-be-fired bus driver slept.

CHEWING CLEATS

Buddy Hunter sunk his teeth into an argument on May 13, 1980. Hunter, the Single-A Winston-Salem Red Sox manager, grabbed a baseball from the dugout after a disputed home run call, ran onto the field, threw the ball against the right field wall, raced back to the infield, slid into first base, ripped off his shoes, and gnawed on them for a few minutes. He was ejected.

IMPROMPTU INFIELD

The Single-A Florence Blue Jays' bus broke down at 2:30 a.m. on the way home from a road trip in the early 1980s. The stranded players were milling around outside a grocery store when manager Dennis Holmberg put them to work. Holmberg had the team stretch, grab their gloves, and spread out for a late-night practice in the grocery store parking lot.

STOLEN BASE

Durham Bulls manager Bobby Dews ripped second base out of the ground and threw it into the stands during an argument with a Single-A Carolina League umpire on May 28, 1982. He also kicked the rosin bag in the air.

RETURN ON INVESTMENT

Joe Buzas owned parts or all of 69 different minor league teams over a 35-year period. He bought the Double-A Reading Phillies for $1 in 1976 and sold the team for $1 million in 1987.

FIRST BASE IS ORANGE

Single-A Columbia Mets manager Butch Hobson was ejected from a 1987 game after arguing a call at first base. Hobson yanked the base out of the ground and took it to the clubhouse in protest. Columbia's general manager entered the locker room and told Hobson he needed the base back to continue the game. Hobson grabbed a can of orange spray paint, sprayed the base bright orange, ran onto the field, pounded the base into its spot, and asked the umpire if the highlighted base was easier to see.

AUTOGRAPHED

Hobson had a signature ejection when managing the independent Nashua Pride in 2000. He got tossed from a game, ripped second base out of the ground, brought it off the field, signed the base, and handed it to a kid.

WHO'S THE BOSS?

The Triple-A Nashville Sounds had five different managers in 1988. Opening day manager Jack Lind left the team at mid-season because of health issues and was replaced, temporarily, by pitching coach Wayne Garland. Garland was succeeded by veteran manager George Scherger, who worked one game, had second thoughts, and went back into retirement. Jim Hoff replaced Scherger before accepting a job in the Cincinnati Reds' front office. Former MLB manager Frank Lucchesi was the fifth and final skipper that season in Music City.

THE MASCOT IS MANAGING

On June 29, 1989, Boise Hawks manager Mal Fichman was ejected after arguing a close play. When he retreated to the clubhouse, he found a man in the Humphrey the Hawk mascot suit sitting in there for the air conditioning. After telling the man to take a break, Fichman put on the mascot suit, walked into the dugout, and managed the rest of the game by whispering decisions to his hitting coach.

Northwest League president Jack Cain was at the game, noticed the mascot was wearing spikes, and connected the dots. Fichman was suspended for one game.

DOME

Bruce Bochy has a big head, literally. Bochy managed San Diego Padres minor league affiliates from 1989–1992 and his teams had to order specially made hats to fit his size $8^{1/8}$ head.

SUMO SKIPPERS

Fargo's Doug Simunic and St. Paul's Marty Scott got tossed from the same independent Northern League game in 1996 and the two managers hatched a plan under the grandstand. They slipped into inflatable sumo wrestler suits, walked onto the field, and bounced against each other between innings. The umpire identified Simunic and Scott and ejected them again.

SUBSTITUTE TEACHER

The list of Pioneer League managers in 1993 included former major leaguers Paul Runge and John Shelby, and a teacher. Ernest Rodriguez was a teacher in southern California but the Pioneer League's short-season schedule allowed him to move to Idaho for the summer and manage the Pocatello Posse. Pocatello general manager John Stein went from the front office to the dugout and managed the final seven games that year when Rodriguez reported to school.

PRIME TIME

Broadcast legends Bob Costas and Larry King were the celebrity managers for the 1993 Double-A All-Star Game in Memphis, Tennessee. Costas's team won, winning him the right to write King's *USA Today* column for a week. Costas was also jokingly ejected from the game.

OUTRAGED OWNER

After an umpire mistakenly called an opposing foul ball a home run in 1993, Sioux Falls Canaries owner George Stavrenos jumped out of his seat, ran down the aisle, hopped over the railing, bustled onto the field, and screamed at the umpire while waving his hands. The independent Northern League suspended Stavrenos for the rest of the season.

BLOCKBUSTER TRADE

Pitcher Kerry Ligtenberg was traded for twelve dozen baseballs and two dozen bats in 1996. Ligtenberg was with the independent Minneapolis Loons of the Prairie League when the Atlanta Braves scouted him and liked what they saw. The Braves offered cash for Ligtenberg, but the Loons were short on baseballs and bats, so they asked for those instead.

DRY OFF!

Canton Crocodiles manager Dan Massarelli tried to make a mid-inning pitching change in 1999 but the move went down the drain. Massarelli took the ball from his starter, who walked off the field, undressed in the clubhouse, and started showering. But the incoming reliever wasn't on Canton's lineup card and was ineligible to pitch. The starter got out of the shower, put his uniform back on, raced back onto the field, and got the final two outs of the inning.

POTTY BREAK

Single-A Asheville Tourists manager Joe Mikulik was ejected from a home game on June 9, 2000. Before he went to the clubhouse, he protested his ejection by placing a toilet near the first base line.

VICTORY LAP

Moments before the Triple-A Salt Lake Buzz gave away a motorcycle on the field after their win on April 29, 2000, the team's manager Phil Roof took it for a test drive. Roof mounted the bike, revved it up, and rode it most of the way around the bases, but he fell turning at third. His players jokingly surrounded the scene of the crash with police tape the next day.

FOOL IN THE RAIN

Famed Single-A Charleston RiverDogs owner Bill Murray made the tarp his stage on June 10, 2012. Fans were waiting through a rain delay when Murray ran around the tarp, slid head-first over home plate, then high-fived players in the dugout.

SLUMBER PARTY

The Vermont Expos' staff saw the sun rise above Centennial Field seven mornings in a row in 2003. The Expos were struggling through a five-game losing streak and the team's general manager C. J. Knudsen agreed to sleep in the dugout until his team won a game, with an additional staff member joining him after each loss. With an overcrowded dugout, and interns sleeping on the roof, the Expos finally won a game, ending their losing streak at 12, and sending the front office back to their own beds.

WEATHER ISSUES

Boise Hawks manager Jody Davis pulled his team off the field in Everett, Washington, after his left fielder slipped on wet grass while chasing a fly ball on August 7, 2010. Davis felt the field was unplayable because of an earlier rainstorm, but the umpires felt the field was fine. The umpires told Davis that his team had five minutes to take the field, but Davis continued the protest. Five minutes passed and Everett was handed a forfeit win.

LIVING HIS DREAM

At the peak of his *Saturday Night Live* fame, Murray played minor league baseball. In 1978, the show asked its contributors to take up their dream job, and Murray selected professional baseball player for his occupation. Murray's business manager owned the independent Grays Harbor Loggers of the Northwest League and signed him to a contract. The 27-year-old Murray went 1-for-2 in his two professional games.

HEY BRO

Minnesota Twins star Joe Mauer rehabbed for four games in 2014 with the Twins' Single-A Cedar Rapids affiliate, where his brother Jake was the manager.

LATER BRO

On June 20, 1997, the Cincinnati Reds demoted infielder Bret Boone to Triple-A Indianapolis and called up his brother Aaron to replace him.

FILL IN THE BLANKS

Luis Rivera, the manager of the Appalachian League's Kingsport Mets, forgot to write some of his relief pitchers on his lineup card on June 26, 2015, making them ineligible for that night's game against Bluefield. The Mets had to bring in position players to pitch and a close game turned into a 15-8 Mets loss.

A WORK OF ART

When managing the Double-A Mobile BayBears in 2017, Sal Fasano spent 40 minutes before each game writing his players' names in calligraphy on the lineup card. He's a self-taught calligraphist who buys his preferred pens, ink, and card stock at craft stores.

LIKE FATHER, LIKE SON

Rocket Wheeler managed the New York-Penn League's Auburn Doubledays in 2019, his 27th season as a minor league manager. His son, who's nicknamed "Missile," sometimes worked as his bullpen catcher.

NOT MASKING HIS ANGER

Minor league managers had to wear masks early in the 2021 season as a pandemic precaution. Triple-A Reno manager Blake Lalli moved his mask over his eyes and mimicked strike calls during an on-field argument with the home plate umpire on May 14, 2021. He was ejected.

PYRO PALATE

Southern Illinois Miners manager Mike Pinto eats fire. Pinto winters as a motivational speaker and as part of his presentation he lights a stick on fire and puts it in his mouth. His presentation seems to work with his players too; through 2021, the independent Miners posted winning records in 12 of Pinto's 13 seasons there.

RYNO

The Tennessee Smokies' ballpark has an aisle called "Sandberg Alley" because that's where Hall of Famer Ryne Sandberg signed autographs for lines of fans when he managed the Double-A Smokies in 2009.

UMPIRES & LEAGUES

YEAR-ROUND

In 1885, the California State League started its season on January 4 and ended it on December 27. Teams played once a week.

DRY DUGOUTS

California League directors approved a policy in 1886 that prohibited players from buying alcoholic drinks at ballparks during games.

PETITION

The Southern League set a rule in 1886 saying umpires would be removed from the league if four different teams protested their performance.

FESTIVE

There were parades across the Texas League in the late 1800s. Players often left their home or hotel and marched to the ballpark in full uniform to drum up support for that day's game.

DOUBLE AGENT

Harry "Bird Eye" Truby was blacklisted for baseball bigamy. Truby signed two Texas League contracts for 1890–one to manage Austin and one to play for Fort Worth. The Texas League investigated and banned Truby for life.

NORTH DAKOTA NOTHING

Fargo and Grand Forks endured 25 scoreless innings on July 18, 1891, setting the still-active record for longest professional game without a run scored. The Red River Valley League umpire ended the game after 25 innings because both teams had to catch a train.

HOME SWEET HOME

In the nineteenth century, multiple minor leagues allowed home teams to bat first. Some teams did, sending visitors to the field for the top of the first inning.

GOTTA ASK FIRST

On May 16, 1896, Texas Association umpire Ed Clark ejected a groundskeeper from the Paris vs. Waco game for brushing off home plate without his permission.

SEXTUPLE-HEADER

The Portland Phenoms and Manchester Manchesters played six games in one day in 1899. The Manchesters were chasing the first place Newport Colts in the second half standings and the Colts slyly scheduled a doubleheader to try and seal a first place finish. Manchester reacted by scheduling six games on the final day, with the first contest starting at 9 a.m. The plan seemed to work–the Manchesters won all six games and seemingly finished in first place, but New England League officials later decided only two of the six wins counted and Newport was declared the second half champion.

BAD HAIR DAY

New York State League umpire John Conroy ejected Binghamton Bingoes manager Jack Calhoun from an early 1900s game because Calhoun made a joke about Conroy's hair.

PRIZEFIGHTER

Jim Jeffries was the toughest umpire in baseball on May 24, 1900. Jeffries was the heavyweight champion of the world when the New York State League hired him to umpire the Schenectady vs. Albany game. More than 4,000 fans came out to see him.

OUTSIDE INFLUENCE

New York State League umpire Bill Klem ended a game from the parking lot in 1903 when the Binghamton Bingoes' owner locked him out of the stadium after a bad call. Bingoes management refused to let Klem back in, so he handed Binghamton a forfeit loss.

FOOTBALL TOSS

A player named Williams was ejected from a 1903 Class B Utica Pent-Ups game for "using Umpire Downer as a football."

WALKOUT

The umpiring conditions were so bad in the Class D Hudson River League in 1903 that all of the league's umpires resigned by June 21.

SECRETARY'S DAY

An employee mistake made Texas League stats incomplete in 1903. The league secretary lost all box scores from the first half of the season, so league leaders were based only on players' second half performances.

THERE'S NO PLACE LIKE HOME

An American Association umpire named Stone left during the 1905 season because he was homesick.

SINISTER PLOT

Two Milwaukee players brewed a plan to hurt an umpire on June 10, 1905. Pitcher Jack Hickey conspired with catcher Roland Wolfe to have Wolfe intentionally miss a high fastball so it would hit the umpire in the head. The umpire gave opposing Indianapolis a forfeit win when he caught wind of the plan hatched by Milwaukee's battery.

PRAY FOR UMPIRES

Fans were growing impatient in Poughkeepsie, New York, on June 12, 1905, because the umpire didn't show up. The Class C Poughkeepsie Colts were ready to play the Paterson Intruders while team management was trying to find the absent umpire. Local Reverend C. S. Rahm appeared from the stands and offered to umpire the game without bias. The teams agreed, he officiated the game, and everyone was pleased with the reverend's performance.

SCRAMBLED

Umpires today are barked at from the stands and criticized online, but that's nothing compared to the mess a minor league umpire named Kane dealt with. On August 17, 1905, Kane made a call in Toledo, Ohio, against the home team and fans bombarded him with eggs and mud. Security arrived as he was blitzed with flying seat cushions. Police guarded the battered umpire on his postgame walk to the hotel.

SICK DAYS

The Class D Kentucky-Illinois-Tennessee League terminated its 1905 season on August 17 because of a yellow fever epidemic. Some clubs later admitted their cities didn't have an outbreak but they agreed to the cancellation to save money.

A FRUIT OR A VEGETABLE?

Umpire Brick Owens made a bad call in Minneapolis in July 1906 and thousands of vengeful fans pelted Owens with tomatoes early in the next day's game. The shower of produce created such a mess that Owens forfeited the game to visiting Columbus.

PICKPOCKET

When Class B Central League umpire Cy Rigler got into a fight with South Bend Greens first baseman Buck Connors in the third inning of a game on July 22, 1906, South Bend fans swarmed the field to help Connors. As if Rigler's bumps and bruises weren't enough, someone stole $215 from him during the ruckus.

RUNAWAYS

A New England League umpire fled the Worcester vs. Fall River game in the middle of the fourth inning on August 25, 1906. The umpire, named Langdon, made a questionable call regarding a batted ball being lost in tall outfield grass and the fans began shouting threats at him. Langdon snuck under the grandstand, removed his chest protector, and took off, leaving a cloud of dust in the street behind him.

He wasn't the last umpire to escape mid-game. During a 1938 Class D Arizona-Texas League game in El Paso, Texas, the home plate umpire took off his mask, put down his chest protector, walked off the field, and never returned.

HAVE A BALL

The Mobile Sea Gulls' celebration was short-lived after a 1907 win over Vicksburg. The Class D Cotton States League yanked the game from the standings because the teams didn't use an official Spalding baseball.

FOUL LANGUAGE

Class C Virginia League umpire William Hoffner was arrested and fined $5 for using improper language during the Richmond vs. Lynchburg game on July 3, 1907.

Class D Fond du Lac Webfoots first baseman Albert Spanton was arrested and locked up in county jail in August 1907 for using vulgar language during a road game in Wausau, Wisconsin.

EYECHART

Fans couldn't accuse New England League umpires of having bad eyesight in 1907. The Class B league made umpires show a valid vision certificate from an optometrist before working a game.

WILD WEST

Former Wisconsin State League president James Powers volunteered to umpire a game in Nevada in August 1907. Powers wasn't comfortable in an unfamiliar area, so he showed up with a revolver on his belt. Local sheriffs disarmed him before the game.

EASY AS ONE, TWO, THREE

An umpire lost track of outs in a 1908 Class D game in Meridian, Mississippi, and he chose an interesting way to make up for his mistake. After erroneously giving a team four outs one inning, the ump announced that team would get only two outs in the next inning. The Cotton States League nullified the game after learning of the umpire's addition and subtraction.

PICKUP GAME

A Class D contest ended with bases in the outfield. Heavy rain interrupted the Cotton States League game in Vicksburg, Mississippi, on August 4, 1908, and flooded the infield dirt. An umpire named Laroque determined the outfield grass was playable so he arranged the bases in the outfield and the teams finished the game out there.

LICENSE AND REGISTRATION PLEASE

When an umpire named Brennan arrived to work a Class A game in Des Moines, Iowa, on August 21, 1908, Des Moines Boosters president John Higgins insisted that Brennan show his credentials. Brennan refused, so Higgins ordered police officers to arrest him. The umpire had the last laugh–Brennan ruled a forfeit loss to Des Moines as he was being dragged away by police.

WITHDRAWAL

The Class D Kansas State League game between Lyons and McPherson lasted 21 innings on July 27, 1909. It also included a craving delay, when the umpire paused the eighteenth inning to ask the dugouts for some chewing tobacco.

ARMED ARGUMENT

Class D Ohio State League umpire L.S. Raphun pulled a gun on a fan in Lancaster, Ohio, on June 29, 1910. The fan was heckling Raphun before the game about a call the previous day and Raphun approached the fan. The fan slapped Raphun, so Raphun yanked out his revolver and threatened to shoot. The police arrived and arrested the umpire but he was set free until his court hearing. Raphun went back to the ballpark, worked the game, and kept his gun concealed.

HURRY UP

The Southern Association demanded that every team play as fast as possible on September 19, 1910, as an experiment, more than a century before MLB instituted pace-of-play tests in the minors.

GO DOWN SWINGING

Caruthersville and Paragould fought to the end. The two Class D clubs and their fans brawled during the decisive game of the 1910 Northeast Arkansas League Championship Series, so the umpires stopped play. The teams couldn't agree on when to complete the playoffs, so the series ended in a tie.

AROUND THE HORN

Class D Blue Grass League players weren't allowed to throw the ball around the infield between innings or after outs in 1911. League president William Neal felt those traditions prolonged games and he threatened fines for any players violating the rule.

NO DAYS OFF

In 1911, Class B Three-I League teams played 140 games in 138 days.

PAST DUE

An unpaid bill has kept the 1911 Class C Minnesota-Wisconsin League stats incomplete for more than a century. The official scorer in Duluth, Minnesota, refused to submit his box scores until he got paid. His paycheck never came, so neither did his box scores.

SO YOU THINK YOU CAN UMPIRE

Central Association president M. E. Justice was tired of fans in Keokuk, Iowa, constantly complaining about umpires. He challenged fans to try it themselves, offering $20 to anybody willing to umpire a Class D game there. Local government employee Hiram Stebbins accepted the challenge and umpired the game on June 24, 1911, to both teams' satisfaction.

ENTHUSIASM

Class D Illinois-Missouri League umpire Dit Spencer swung his arm so fiercely making an out call in 1912 that he dislocated his shoulder and had to see a doctor.

ROYAL RUMBLE

The Class D Tulsa Terriers accused umpire A. W. McKee of being intoxicated before their game on June 5, 1912. McKee didn't take the criticism well and fought Tulsa's owner, both managers, and two players. The scrappy umpire was taken to jail and a replacement ump was found in the stands.

PRESIDENTIAL PLAYER

Connecticut League president and Hall of Famer Jim O'Rourke strapped on a catcher's mask and played for the Class B New Haven Murlins at age 62 on September 14, 1912. O'Rourke was visiting New Haven for the Murlins' season-ending doubleheader and he volunteered to help the fatigued team by catching Game 1. He caught all nine innings, 19 years after his last full season in the majors.

THAT ESCALATED QUICKLY

In 1914, Fort Worth Panthers players surrounded Texas League umpire Ben Doyle and pushed him down after a contested call. After the game, Doyle walked into Fort Worth's clubhouse with a pistol and pointed it at each player individually, demanding an apology. Every player apologized.

YOUR CALL

Southern League umpire Scotty Chestnut let New Orleans batter Red Bluhm make a call one day in the mid-1910s. A gust of wind blew dust into Chestnut's eyes as a pitch was coming in, so he didn't see its location.

"How did the ball look to you, Red?" Chestnut asked.

"It looked like a ball," Bluhm replied.

"Ball three!" Chestnut declared.

THIRD WHEEL

The Tri-Copper League pulled off an unimaginable schedule from 1915–1917. It had only three teams, leaving one squad without an opponent every game day.

UP THE CREEK WITHOUT A PADDLE

Florida State League umpire Tiny Parker got thrown into the Halifax River after a Daytona Beach Islanders home game in the early 1920s. The Islanders' ballpark was surrounded by water, so Parker had to walk over a bridge after the game to get back to his hotel. A group of angry fans surrounded him and threw him off the bridge. He swam out of the deep river but lost his suitcase with his umpiring gear inside. The fans were so impressed that Parker showed up the next day that they collected money and bought him new equipment and a new suitcase.

MAN OF THE PEOPLE

Jack Wilkinson umpired from an unexpected vantage point during a 1920s Class A Western Association game. Wilkinson was tired of fans heckling him, so he turned around and yelled, "If you can see the pitches better than I can from up there, then I'm obviously in the wrong place." He then climbed into the stands and called balls and strikes while sitting with the jeering fans.

FARM TEAMS

The Class B Three-I League shut down early in 1917, ending the season on July 8 because of fertile soil. It was an especially promising yield of crops that year throughout the Midwest and many players wanted to take advantage.

BUG SPRAY

The Wilson Bugs' 1921 Class B Virginia League championship got squished by MLB commissioner Kenesaw Mountain Landis because the Bugs violated the league salary cap.

BUSTER'S BUCKET

Hopkinsville's Buster Brown rubbed chewing tobacco in a Kentucky-Illinois-Tennessee League umpire's face after a bad call in 1922. With tobacco juice stinging his eyes, the Class D umpire begged for help. That's when Brown dumped a bucket of water on the ump's head. Brown was arrested for disturbing the peace.

DISBARRED

The entire city of Norfolk, Virginia, was banished from professional baseball after a mob of fans there attacked an umpire named Harper on August 30, 1923. The city and Norfolk Tars baseball club applied for reinstatement the next year and the National Association of Professional Baseball Leagues allowed the Tars to rejoin the Class B Virginia League.

ELECTION

The 1923 Class D North Dakota League season ended early because of financial difficulties, but the league still wanted to crown a champion, so they held a vote among executives and declared the Minot Magicians champions.

DEDUCTIBLE

Muskogee Athletics player Alabama Jones was ordered to pay umpire J.W. Wilkinson's medical bills and salary after Jones kicked Wilkinson during a Class C Western Association game in 1924.

SAN ANTONIO'S MISSION

The visiting Fort Worth Panthers were given a forfeit victory on May 21, 1925, when San Antonio Bears fans emptied the stands, rushed onto the field, and mobbed the umpire in the fifth inning.

ROOM SERVICE

Milwaukee first baseman Guy Griffin and American Association umpire George Magerkurth argued fiercely during a game in Indianapolis on April 24, 1927. Their fight was revived a few hours later at a hotel and punches were thrown. Magerkurth broke Griffin's shoulder and was sentenced to a month in jail.

THE CHAIR WAS MADE OF IRON!

A rabid fan in El Paso, Texas, threw a chair and hit home plate umpire Pug Cavet in the head on July 5, 1931. The fan was upset about Cavet's strike zone.

YARD SALE

In 1935, longtime minor league umpire Harry "Steamboat" Johnson published a book about his career and brought copies to ballparks to sell to fans before games. One day in Mobile, Alabama, Johnson made a bad call and dozens of books came flying down from the stands. He had the batboy collect all of the books so he could sell them the next day in another city.

NEAT FREAKS

The Class B Elmira Red Wings won $400 from the New York-Penn League in 1932 for being the team that showed "the most hustling abilities and neatest appearance on the field."

MAKE UP YOUR MIND

Sportswriters called it the "Play of Six Decisions." Minneapolis center fielder Harry Rice made a diving backhand catch in the ninth inning of Game 6 of the 1932 Junior World Series and Newark manager Al Marmaux argued the ball hit the ground. The umpires got together and reversed the call, then switched it back. Then they changed their minds three more times as players, managers, and fans reacted to each repeal. The discussion and all of its develop-ments took 40 minutes.

A CHARACTER

Between 1911 and 1946, Steamboat Johnson worked more minor league games than any umpire in history. He ran and slid next to base runners to get a closer view, opened boxes of baseballs with his teeth, and bellowed the starting lineups while waving his arms. He traveled with an optometrist certificate to show to fans who ques-tioned his eyesight.

THUMB'S DOWN

Minor league umpire Chester Widerquist couldn't avoid confronta-tion, even in the off-season. Widerquist wintered as a bartender in Illinois and on January 1, 1938, he tried to eject a drunk patron from his saloon. The customer fought Widerquist and bit off part of his thumb. The biter was charged with disorderly conduct and Wider-quist returned to ballparks in 1939 with a wild story to tell.

A TIE BALL?

A minor league umpire in the South couldn't decide if a close 3-2 pitch was a ball or a strike during a tense inning in the late 1930s, so he called the pitch a "tie ball" and made the pitcher throw another pitch. The batter grounded out.

WHITE ON WHITE

In 1938, the Class C Mid-Atlantic League experimented with white stitches on white baseballs to make the ball more visible during night games. The experiment ended after just one season.

DON'T IGNORE ME

On August 25, 1938, in Goldsboro, North Carolina, Coastal Plain League umpire W.T. Chewning gave the Class D Goldsboro Goldbugs a forfeit loss because they were ignoring his requests for new baseballs.

BLADE

Texas League umpire William Wilson was suspended 90 games in 1939 for pulling a knife on players who were harassing him during a San Antonio-Fort Worth game.

NOW **JACK CORBETT'S** "WORLD FAMOUS" HOLLYWOOD BASE SETS

ALL ABOUT THAT BASE

Minor leaguer Jack Corbett never touched a major league field, but his bases did. Corbett played from 1908–1917 and found bases to be too loose. He created bases with a stem to insert below ground for increased stability and called his invention "Jack Corbett Hollywood Base Sets." Major League Baseball picked up his patent in 1939 and Corbett's concoction has been MLB's official base ever since.

SOFT LANDING

Quebec Alouettes fans had comfy confrontations with Class C Canadian-American League umpires in the 1940s. When they disagreed with a call, they threw pillows at the ump.

TIME'S UP

Night games were new to minor league baseball in the 1940s and teams were paying costly electric bills to power stadium lights. The *Birmingham News* suggested the Southern Association should limit on-field arguments to 30 seconds as a way to quicken night games and save money.

NO MORE MEETINGS

The Southern Association was trying to streamline pregame routines in 1943 and decided to eliminate the home plate lineup card exchanges between managers and umpires.

READ THE ROOM

In 1946, an American Association umpire thought a game in Indianapolis was tied, so he brushed off home plate in anticipation of extra innings. The game wasn't tied; it ended at the conclusion of the ninth inning.

TELECOMMUTING

Edwin Johnson was a president and a senator at the same time. Johnson was president of the Class A Western League from 1947–1955 while representing Colorado in the U. S. Senate.

EXPOSED

Three-I League umpire Gene Allinger put himself in danger during a Class B game on August 8, 1947, in Decatur, Illinois. Allinger called balls and strikes on the first two batters before realizing he forgot to wear a mask.

DUST YOURSELF OFF AND TRY AGAIN

One day in the late 1940s, a group of angry fans in Mahanoy City, Pennsylvania, picked up Class D North Atlantic League umpire Patrick Shaner and threw him over the center field fence. While team management searched for a fill-in umpire, Shaner walked through the front gate, cleaned off home plate, and shouted, "Play ball!"

PAID ENDORSER

A Class A Eastern League umpire wore advertisements on his back and chest protector in 1950 before being told that wasn't allowed.

UNDECIDED

The 1950 Class D North Atlantic League Championship Series hasn't finished yet. Game 6 between the Lebanon Chix and Stroudsburg Poconos was rained out and then the league went out of business.

PICK A CARD, ANY CARD

Umpire Frank Drubinka wintered as a night club entertainer who did card tricks, and he used those skills during a Class D Alabama State League game in 1950. A batter argued Drubinka's third strike call and the umpire responded by pulling out a deck of cards and asking the batter to pick one. Drubinka correctly guessed that the card was the seven of spades and told the batter to trust his judgement on everything.

TOOTHLESS

Umpire Al Sample's false teeth fell out while he was making a call at home plate during a Class C Longhorn League game in Artesia, New Mexico, in the early 1950s.

LIE DETECTOR

The International League used polygraph evidence to overturn a suspension on August 10, 1953. The league disciplined Buffalo manager Jack Tighe for spitting on an umpire. Tighe insisted the spitting was unintentional and offered to take a polygraph test. Using the Buffalo Police Department's equipment, Tighe passed the test and the league ended his suspension.

ARBITER

Class B Carolina League umpire Harry Reeder missed a call in July 1954 in Durham, North Carolina, and fans stormed the field. The *Durham Morning Herald* blasted Reeder in an article titled "Incompetent Umpires Always End Up in Rhubarbs." Reeder sued the newspaper and received a financial settlement in 1955.

FOR IT'S ONE, TWO STRIKES YOU'RE OUT

In 1957, the Class D Florida State League voted to give batters a walk after three balls and pitchers a strikeout after two strikes. The plan was in place for the 1958 season until MLB overruled the radical changes.

GROUNDS FOR DISMISSAL

Police had to run on the field after the Houston vs. San Antonio game on August 2, 1958, to break up a fight between San Antonio groundskeeper John Olivera and Double-A Texas League umpire Mike Runyon.

IT'S A DRY HEAT

The Triple-A Pacific Coast League gave the Phoenix Giants a month-long road trip in August 1959 so they could avoid Arizona's scorching summer temperatures.

YOU ARE LOOKING LIVE

Legendary broadcaster Brent Musburger started his sports career as a Class D Midwest League umpire in 1959. He made 26 ejections that year.

AHEAD OF THEIR TIME

In 1959, the Texas League allowed pitchers to signal for an intentional walk without throwing four balls. In 1969, the American Association, Eastern League, International League, New York-Penn League, and Texas League all experimented with different versions of a designated hitter for the pitcher. The Texas League used 20-second pitch clocks from 1963–1964. All of these rules were implemented in the minor leagues before being implemented or seriously considered in the major leagues.

BUZZER BEATERS

The 20-second pitch timers the independent Northern League used in the 1990s blared a loud noise when they expired.

RECENT RULE CHANGES

In 2021, the independent Pioneer League announced games tied after nine innings would be decided by a home run derby. Each team designated a hitter to take five swings and try to out-homer his opponent. The independent Frontier League also replaced extra innings with a home run derby in 2021.

On the pitching side, the independent Atlantic League moved the mound a foot farther from home plate for half of the 2021 season as an MLB-initiated experiment to see if there would be fewer strikeouts from 61 feet, six inches. Also in the Atlantic League, beginning in 2022, batters could try to run to first base on any pitch that isn't caught in the air by the catcher.

OFF THE TOP ROPE

Hefty umpire Ken Kaiser worked minor league games from 1965–1977. He spent two of those off-seasons as a hooded professional wrestler named "The Hatchet."

SLOBBERKNOCKER

Speaking of professional wrestling, Oklahoman and longtime WWE announcer Jim Ross is a friend of the Triple-A Oklahoma City Dodgers. The team sold his JR's BBQ products at its concession stands in recent years.

SERIES SWEEP

Eastern League umpire Ron Luciano ejected Double-A Elmira Pioneers manager Earl Weaver from all four games of a series in 1965.

SPACIOUS

The Gulf Coast League reconfigured their outfield foul lines to widen fair territory by 3 percent in 1970. It was an experiment to create more room for hits to fall in. It led to an average of 100 more hits per team compared to the previous year.

CHIRPING

Jackson Mets player Terry Ervin was thrown out of both games of a Double-A Texas League doubleheader in 1977, and he didn't play a minute in either one. He was tossed twice because of comments he made from the bench.

HOLD MY BEER

Then there was Triple-A Las Vegas outfielder Darrell Ceciliani, who got thrown out of the same game twice on August 3, 2015. He was given an automatic strike for being slow to arrive to the batter's box, argued that call, and was ejected by the home plate umpire. The first base umpire ran in to help calm the argument and, not realizing Ceciliani had already been ejected, also threw him out of the game.

HAWAIIAN SHIRT DAY

In the 1970s, the Triple-A Pacific Coast League allowed its umpires to wear Hawaiian shirts on the field when working Hawaii Islanders home games.

MASS EXODUS

A minor league umpire cleared out an entire major league dugout on May 9, 1979. Triple-A ump Dave Pallone was replacing striking MLB umpires and he made a call at second base in Houston that went against St. Louis. When bats, helmets, and towels were lobbed onto the turf in protest, Pallone ordered everyone in the dugout to go into the clubhouse. After a meeting on the field, Pallone determined only three Cardinals were ejected and the game continued.

FLOWER POWER

George Spelius ran the Single-A Midwest League from a Wisconsin floral shop in the 1980s. The league president/florist had two phone lines–one for flower orders and one for Midwest League business.

CAUGHT STEALING

Single-A Carolina League umpires Frank Nieves and Pete DeFlesco were fired in 1983 for stealing baseballs.

NO DICE

Minor league executives gambled and lost by scheduling the 1984 Triple-A World Series in Las Vegas. MLB commissioner Bowie Kuhn cancelled the event because of concerns over casinos sponsoring it and people gambling on it.

SIBLING RIVALRY

Nick Bevington was striving to be a major league umpire at the same time his brother Terry was climbing the minor league managing ladder, and there was no favoritism when they worked the same series. Nick ejected Terry from a 1985 Double-A Texas League game for arguing.

THE CHARLESTON DANCE

Single-A South Atlantic League standings were confusing between 1987 and 2004, when the circuit had two teams with "Charleston" in their names. Charleston, South Carolina, and Charleston, West Virginia, played each other at least one series per year. The standings became less confusing in 2005, when the Charleston Alley Cats rebranded as the "West Virginia Power."

MESSAGE RECEIVED

New York-Penn League umpire Steve McMullen ejected the Mahoning Valley Scrappers' scoreboard operator from a 2001 game for flashing a disapproving "Booo" on the scoreboard's message screen after a call against the home team.

CORRUPT JUDGES

Players became umpires in a 2003 Midwest League game in Cedar Rapids, Iowa. At the Single-A level, there are only two umpires assigned to each game, so when Buzz Laird left the Lansing vs. Cedar Rapids game with heat exhaustion on August 25, 2003, his partner Brian Reilly asked a player from each team to serve as base umpires. The biased players did not make objective decisions. Lansing's Ryan O'Malley ignored a balk by his teammate and Cedar Rapids' Jake Mathis gave a tentative safe sign on a play at first base in the twelfth inning, helping his team win the game.

More than a century earlier, players had to officiate a Savannah vs. Atlanta game in 1886 because the scheduled umpire, a man named McQuade, didn't show up for the game on the same day he was followed by a private detective.

GARBAGE TIME

Frisco's Engel Beltre was suspended 15 games by the Double-A Texas League for throwing a trash can at fans above the dugout after a close loss in San Antonio on April 26, 2011. Two rowdy fans were arrested in the altercation.

NO UMPS ALLOWED

The independent St. Paul Saints scheduled an exhibition game without umpires in 2013. Catchers called balls and strikes, fielders determined if batted balls went fair or foul, and groups of Little Leaguers with front row seats ruled plays on the basepaths.

NICE TO MEET YOU

Minor league umpires went on strike in 2006 and some of the replacement umpires weren't qualified. When a Double-A Texas League batter fouled off a pitch and the catcher reached his hand back to get a new baseball, the umpire shook the catcher's hand.

BANNED FOR BALKS

Oakland A's minor league instructor Todd Steverson was suspended one year by the California League after losing a game on purpose. Steverson was managing the High-A Stockton Ports in a marathon game in Modesto, California, on June 23, 2012. Stockton ran out of pitchers and Steverson was forced to put outfielder Josh Whitaker on the mound. In both the seventeenth and eighteenth innings, Steverson asked Whitaker to balk on purpose to move Modesto runners into scoring position. The game ended on a single by Modesto's Helder Velazquez after an intentional balk moved the winning run to third base.

PLEASE HOLD

In 2014, Triple-A umpires stopped a game in El Paso, Texas, to call the press box and ask what the count was. In 2016, Double-A umpires stopped a game in Biloxi, Mississippi, and left the field to check the rulebook after a strange play.

MERGER

The independent American Association had an odd number of teams in 2016, so it combined two clubs into one. The Amarillo Thunderheads and Grand Prairie Air-Hogs used the same roster, with both cities and ballparks getting 25 home games instead of 50.

IN STITCHES

The High-A California League game between Inland Empire and Lake Elsinore on June 27, 2016, had a mid-game, five-minute delay when base umpire Ryan Powers split his pants, called time, walked off the field, and put on new pants.

THE ONE-EYED UMPIRE

Despite an injury that required the removal of an eye, Max McCleary umpired in the independent Frontier League from 1995–2005. He was inducted into the league's Hall of Fame in 2016.

BATHROOM BREAK

Boise's 20-inning win over Eugene in Eugene, Oregon, on July 4, 2017, was delayed for eight minutes when an umpire had to use the bathroom late in the marathon game.

AN UMP'S ASSIST

On April 22, 2018, Triple-A Gwinnett's Rio Ruiz came to bat in Pawtucket, Rhode Island, with runners at first and second and no outs. He smacked a ground ball off first base, past the first baseman, and off the first base umpire. Pawtucket first baseman Sam Travis caught the ricochet off the ump and started a 3-1-6-2, umpire-assisted, triple play.

BAGGED

The Triple-A Pacific Coast League was known for having the toughest travel in baseball prior to schedule modifications in 2021. Teams were sometimes flying more than 1,000 miles on the day of a night game. Games were occasionally postponed because of travel delays or luggage issues.

BUCKLE UNDER PRESSURE

Home plate umpire Takahito Matsuda broke his belt while arguing with Triple-A Louisville batter Alfredo Rodriguez on June 25, 2021. While putting on a replacement belt he borrowed from another umpire, Matsuda ejected Louisville manager Pat Kelly.

LONG-TERM RELATIONSHIP

The uniform number 50 is retired for all High-A South Atlantic League franchises in honor of former league president John Henry Moss, who ran the league for 50 years.

GOING STAG

Only one fan showed up to the Allentown vs. Lancaster game in Lancaster, Pennsylvania, on May 27, 1885, because the game started at the same time as a popular parade nearby.

MAKING THE ROUNDS

Boxing champion Jim Corbett played for 13 different minor league teams in 1897. He joined clubs for a couple days at a time, filling ballparks and receiving half of the ticket revenue. On September 5, fans in Youngstown, Ohio, urged Corbett to leave the field and join a fight in the stands, but he politely declined.

PROTECTIVE CUSTODY

Cortland Wagonmakers fans circled the wagons around Class C New York State League umpire A.M. Gifford after a game in 1900. After Gifford forfeited Cortland's home game to Albany, more than 300 fans surrounded Gifford and he got kicked and slapped until a police officer stuffed him in a ticket office for safety.

MAN OF THE PEOPLE

Bobby Quinn went door-to-door to save the Class A Columbus Senators in 1900. He was the team's business manager and business wasn't good, so Quinn knocked on doors in Columbus, Ohio, selling household supplies to help the team's bottom line. While pitching brooms and brushes, he also pitched baseball, urging residents to attend Senators games. His campaign worked, and within five years Columbus was among the top drawing minor league teams.

SCALPERS

Two Schenectady Frog Alleys players were arrested on May 31, 1903, for selling tickets to a Class B New York State League game that took place the week before.

CLOCKING IN MEMPHIS

Class A Nashville shortstop Dennis Downey was arrested on July 19, 1904, for throwing his bat at noisy fans in Memphis, Tennessee.

FLAT TAX

There was a time when leagues set universal ticket prices and the rate was low. Admission to all Class A Pacific Coast League games increased from 25 cents to 35 cents in 1905. That same year in the Class A Western League, the Denver Grizzlies and Pueblo Indians raised their ticket prices from 25 cents to 30 cents to make up for an increase in travel costs.

PREFERRED CUSTOMER

In the early 1900s, Class A Pacific Coast League umpires announced pregame lineups to the crowd. When only one fan showed up to watch a 1905 Portland vs. Oakland game in Oakland, California, he received personal treatment. The ump bellowed a welcome of "Dear Sir" before introducing both teams.

WITH A LITTLE HELP FROM MY FRIENDS

The American Association's Kansas City Blues were playing an exhibition in El Paso, Texas, in 1908 when a player named Miller fell to the ground due to exhaustion after crossing home plate. A group of fans went on the field, picked up Miller, and carried him to the bench.

COOPED UP

Some San Francisco Seals fans wanted to be behind bars. Recreation Park in San Francisco opened a "Booze Cage" section in 1915. The field-level seating area gave fans free whiskey and beer for their 75-cent entry fee and it was surrounded by wired fencing to separate the carousers from polite fans. Men who sat in the "Booze Cage" shouted at players and started fistfights with each other. Women weren't allowed.

RAW MEAT

Class A Western Association players referred to heckling fans as "wolves" in 1917. A player in that league brought raw hamburger meat into the dugout one day, lobbed handfuls of it at yelling spectators, and told teammates he was "feeding the wolves."

GAME OF TELEPHONE

Some Nashville fans climbed past ticket prices in the 1920s. A telephone pole platform towered above the Sulphur Dell ballpark and kids scaled the pole, sat on the platform, and watched games for free.

MOTORCADE

U. S. President William Taft watched the Class A Denver Grizzlies play on October 3, 1911, becoming the first sitting president to attend a minor league baseball game. His driver parked on the field to give Taft an unobstructed view.

Eighty years later, U. S. President George H. W. Bush attended a High-A Frederick Keys home game in Maryland during his presidency.

BEHIND THE CURTAIN

Gene Martin, general manager of the Class C Akron Yankees in Ohio, didn't like how many people were gathering on the hill behind his ballpark's outfield wall to watch games for free in 1935, so he bought a 200-foot canvas fence and put it atop the outfield wall to block the view of freeloading fans.

RIOT ACT

A sleazy play in Bisbee, Arizona, caused a fan uprising one day in an early 1930s Class D game. El Paso's Mule Washburn pushed a Bisbee runner off second base, tagged him, and got credit for the out. Bisbee fans were so upset at the cheap play and missed call that they stormed the field during the game.

STICKS

Lacrosse was the most popular sport in Cornwall, Ontario, in the 1930s, so the Class C Cornwall Bisons held baseball/lacrosse doubleheaders to sell more tickets.

MUDBALLS

Umpire James Rue said fans in an unnamed Class A Western League city wouldn't let him take cover under the grandstand during a rain delay in 1936. They pushed him back onto the field and threw balls of mud at him.

FROZEN

When fans in Chattanooga, Tennessee, stood on the warning track during overcrowded Chattanooga Lookouts games in 1936, the team froze the game balls to make them travel less far, so the on-field fans were less likely to get hit by a batted ball.

POLLING

It was 1 a.m. and in the nineteenth inning on July 8, 1938, when the umpires in the Fulton vs. Paducah Class D game called time, turned around, faced the grandstand, and asked the fans if the game should continue. The spectators unanimously voted "yes" and Fulton won in the twentieth inning.

AND A PARTRIDGE IN A PEAR TREE

When unconventional owner Bill Veeck took over the American Association's Milwaukee Brewers in 1941, he gave fans random gifts like eels, geese, ladders, lobsters, mice, pigeons, pigs, and a block of ice.

LOST IN THE MAIL

More than 3,000 fans got free admission to the San Francisco Seals' exhibition on March 6, 1949, because the team's ticket stock didn't arrive before the game.

COUPLE

Two Class A Flint Arrows fans had the ballpark to themselves in Flint, Michigan, on September 6, 1951. The official attendance for that night's game was two.

UPSIDE DOWN

The San Francisco Seals hired baseball clown Jackie Price to entertain fans in 1957. Price shot baseballs out of a cannon and caught them while standing on his head.

Price also entertained fans before minor league games in the 1940s by catching fly balls while driving his jeep.

ESCAPE ROOM

Twelve hundred fans were stuck in the ballpark after a Double-A game in Shreveport, Louisiana, on May 8, 1968, when a vandal walked around and locked all of the gates during the game.

RUMOR HAS IT

A prank caller cost the Triple-A Syracuse Chiefs thousands of fans on June 14, 1969. The team was expecting 5,000 people but a hoaxer called a local radio station announcing MacArthur Stadium had been condemned. The false report spread and only 1,300 fans showed up.

GET THEM A TOWEL

Triple-A Eugene Emeralds batter Ruben Amaro hit a foul ball off a grandstand gutter during a 40°F game in Eugene, Oregon, in 1970. The gutter broke and dumped cold water on a section of fans.

HIGH HI

In 1948, Class C Pocatello Cardinals player Ned Sheehan climbed to the top of a light pole during a game and waved to the fans.

SWEET FIELD

The Triple-A Las Vegas Stars' staff scattered chocolate eggs in the outfield for a pregame Easter egg hunt in 1993, but it was a very hot day and the candy melted into a chocolate lake across left field. Las Vegas left fielder D. J. Dozier used a tongue depressor to scrape the chocolate from his cleats during innings and other outfielders reported dizziness from the potent odor of melted chocolate.

FLAMMABLE

The Double-A Savannah Braves distributed deodorant spray cans on Free Deodorant Night in the early 1970s. The team took some heat later when teenage fans lit the aerosol spray and blowtorched some stadium seats.

DEAR GOD

Double-A Savannah Braves general manager Miles Wolff held "Pray for Pitching" night in the 1970s, offering half-price tickets to fans who brought their church bulletin to the box office. Savannah's coaches were offended because they thought the "Pray for Pitching" title was insulting to their pitchers.

WHEN IT RAINS, IT POURS

The wheels came off for the Double-A Birmingham A's one night in 1971. The team lost 8-4 and then raffled off a bike to a kid. When the kid hopped on the bike, the seat broke off and the kid tumbled to the ground.

STANDING ROOM ONLY

The Double-A West Haven Yankees had to stop a game in 1972 because there were too many fans. The team packed 7,200 people into 4,000-seat Quigley Stadium and the fire marshal closed the park because of occupancy laws.

STALLED

The High-A San Bernardino Spirit tried to give away a car between innings on August 29, 1990. Each contestant walked on the field with a key and only one of the keys would start the engine and win the car. The first contestant's key stuck in the ignition, anchoring the car on the warning track. The game was delayed while the Spirit staff pushed the car off the field.

SINGLE

The Double-A Orlando Sun Rays held Blind Date Night in the early 1990s, slotting single women in even-numbered seats and single men in odd-numbered seats. The matchmakers reported mixed results.

FLASH OF GENIUS

The Double-A El Paso Diablos gave away flashlights before a game in 1995 and the public address announcer had an idea. He grabbed his microphone and asked fans to point their flashlights at the opposing pitcher. The hurler was infuriated, as were the umpires, who threatened to eject any fan who turned on their flashlight again.

WHY?

The Double-A Jacksonville Suns booked figure skater Tonya Harding for a ballpark appearance on June 29, 2001, seven years after associates of her ex-husband assaulted fellow skater Nancy Kerrigan's knee with a club. Harding signed mini-bats that were distributed to fans.

BITTER BROWNIE

When the New York-Penn League's New Jersey Cardinals scheduled Brownie Troop Night for June 21, 2002, they didn't think they'd need extra security. The mother of one of the Girl Scouts was so upset about an umpire's call that she bolted from her seat, climbed over the wall, and ran onto the field chasing the umpire. She was ejected and arrested.

SHUT OUT

The Single-A Charleston RiverDogs padlocked the gates before their home game on July 8, 2002. The team purposely banned fans so they could turn in an official attendance of zero to set the professional baseball record for lowest single-game attendance. Some fans peeked above the outfield wall to watch the first few innings atop ladders set up by the team. Once the game became official after five innings, fans were allowed in and kids scrambled to find untouched foul balls in the stands.

SUNRISE START

The independent St. Paul Saints started a game at 5:35 a.m. on May 8, 2005, setting the record for the earliest first pitch in professional baseball history. The Saints scheduled the exhibition game as a Mother's Day promotion and it drew 2,253 sleepy fans. There was a caged rooster on top of the dugout and fans received free cereal. The alarm clocks for the visiting Sioux Falls Canaries chirped at 3:45 a.m. and they were on the field stretching one hour later.

CRIME PAYS

Fresno, California, drivers traded traffic tickets for baseball tickets on April 21, 2007. The Triple-A Fresno Grizzlies held "Second Chance Night" and discounted admission for fans that brought a traffic citation to the ballpark.

A NEW RECORD?

The New York-Penn League's State College Spikes held the "Night of 100 Promotions" on July 28, 2008. The rundown included a paper airplane contest, a paper clip giveaway, a pet rock petting zoo, a rubber band shooting contest, a sock puppet show, a tricycle race, free high-fives, and 93 other promotions.

FILL THE SEATS

Late in the 2009 season, the independent United League announced that the playoff teams with the highest regular season attendance would host their entire first-round series as a way to save on postseason travel costs.

BIG PLAQUE

The New York-Penn League's Lowell Spinners hosted the biggest group-flossing in history on June 29, 2011. The team handed out Glide floss picks and in the fourth inning 3,014 fans worked on their teeth at the same time, minting their place in the Guinness World Records book.

MORE DENTAL HYGIENE

The independent Winnipeg Goldeyes distributed toothbrushes and toothpaste at the gates on June 22, 2005, and when 6,234 fans used the giveaways later in the game, it set the North American record for most people simultaneously brushing their teeth at a professional sporting event. The game was sponsored by the Manitoba Dental Association and included an appearance by the tooth fairy.

CHOPPER

After the Single-A Dayton Dragons set the professional sports record with their 815th consecutive sellout crowd, the team held a celebration on July 23, 2011. Three Cincinnati Reds players, all former Dragons, took a helicopter from Cincinnati to Dayton, Ohio, to be part of the festivities.

DON'T BLOW IT

Fans attending the High-A Dunedin Blue Jays game on May 25, 2012, received a piece of gum and a piece of history. In the fourth inning of the Blue Jays' game against Brevard County, most of the 1,005 fans blew bubble gum bubbles in unison, popping the previous record for most bubbles blown at the same time.

RIDING THE PINE

Someone eating a hot dog or wearing a foam finger in the dugout would normally look unusual, but not at independent San Rafael Pacifics games. The Pacifics offered baseball's first dugout seats in 2013. For $25 each, fans could plop down on the bench next to the players during games.

CORPORAL KLINGER

Actor Jamie Farr made the Triple-A Toledo Mud Hens the most popular minor league team in America in the 1970s by mentioning the club occasionally on the show *M*A*S*H*. Farr was at Toledo's Fifth Third Field on August 25, 2017, for a pregame ceremony inducting Corporal Klinger's character into the ballpark's Celebrity Hall of Fame.

CHILL OUT

The Mud Hens occasionally have a contest where a fan wins a prize if they can sit in a tub of ice water for an entire inning.

PJs

The Single-A Hickory Crawdads held Tribute to Pajamas Night on April 16, 2018. It was National Pajama Day and any fan who showed up in their pajamas got into the game for free.

PASS THE MUSTARD

More than 7,000 St. Paul Saints fans participated in a mid-game food fight on August 14, 2018, in St. Paul, Minnesota. The team planned the edible event to commemorate the fortieth anniversary of the movie *Animal House*. Fans received complimentary ponchos to put on before launching mashed potatoes, marshmallows, popcorn, and other food at each other.

Three years earlier, 6,261 Saints fans set the world record for the largest pillow fight.

CLUNKERS

Various minor league teams have given away old, beaten-up cars over the years, including on August 29, 2014, when the Triple-A Albuquerque Isotopes raffled off the 1994 Buick Century owned by one of their players, Joc Pederson. The Isotopes' description of the car noted that it had "at least one operable window."

TIMBER AND TIMBRE

Montana's Billings Mustangs played in the Pioneer League from 1969 to 2019 and they occasionally booked retired police officer Don Vegge to play the national anthem on his 26-inch steel saw. He used a cello bow to create smooth sounds. Vegge and his saw also performed at Disneyland and released two albums.

TALK TO ME

Phil Salamone was in his thirty-fourth year as a Triple-A Rochester Red Wings usher when the team handed out "Uncle Phil" talking bobbleheads on July 24, 2019, in Rochester, New York. The bobbleheads uttered his familiar phrase: "Uncle Phil loves you!"

ADULTS ONLY

In a reversal of the family-friendly atmosphere in the minor leagues, the Single-A Lake Elsinore Storm held Rated R Night on July 15, 2021, in Lake Elsinore, California. The team press release announcing the theme said there would be "good-natured, adult content all game long" that was "suited for those 18 and older."

BEER ME

The Double-A Bowie Baysox have redefined the phrase "beer run." The team holds an annual 1K Beer Run, where competitors run around the ballpark's warning track three times before a game and receive a free beer after each lap.

HUMAN HOME RUN

Some fans have seen a father and son fly over an outfield fence in recent years. Each summer, David "Cannonball" Smith and his son David "Bullet" Smith Jr. travel the country and shoot themselves out of cannons at carnivals, fairs, and minor league games. Their ballpark blasts shoot them 150 feet and sometimes the netting they land in is set up behind the outfield fence.

YOU ARE TOAST

Rod "Toastman" Blackstone is the most recognizable baseball fan in West Virginia. When an opposing batter strikes out at Charleston Dirty Birds home games, Blackstone starts chants of "you are toast" and flings pieces of burnt toast to fans. The team installed an electrical outlet for "Toastman's" toaster in front of his seat. Blackstone was the deputy Mayor of Charleston but he now works for the team he loves.

ROLLIN' ON THE RIVER

Most fans drive or walk to the ballpark. In Missoula, Montana, fans float to the ballpark. The Missoula PaddleHeads host "Float to the Game" nights, when fans float six miles down the Clark Fork River on rafts and reach land at Ogren Park at Allegiance Field. After unloading, the boaters receive a barbecue meal and a ticket to the game.

BALANCING ACT

Tyler Scheuer is a one-man show who performs at minor league ballparks by balancing bikes, ladders, tables, wheel barrows, and other heavy objects on his chin.

TERRIBLE TRADITION

The Double-A Altoona Curve strive for their worst once a year on "Awful Night." The promotion posts failure averages and baby photos on the scoreboard instead of batting averages and player headshots, launches underwear into the stands in lieu of a T-shirt toss, and distributes useless giveaways like sporks. The romantic "Kiss Cam" is replaced by the solitary "Alone Cam." Meanwhile, "Fan Cam" shows various ceiling and oscillating fans, rather than humans in the stands.

I'M FULL

Nutritionists probably aren't West Michigan Whitecaps fans. The Single-A team's massive Fifth Third Burger includes five beef patties, five slices of cheese, chili, Fritos, salsa, and more. It weighs four pounds and contains 4,800 calories. The Whitecaps have also sold fried Twinkies and fried Pepsi at their concession stands.

POOLSIDE

The Double-A Frisco RoughRiders' lazy river behind their outfield wall is 174 feet long and contains 68,000 gallons of water.

SQUIRRELS LOVE NUTS

Double-A Richmond Flying Squirrels fans know the end of the seventh inning means it's time for the Mixed Nut Race between costumed competitors Johnny Cashew, John Wall-Nut, and Peanut.

NATURE & WILDLIFE

BAAAAD FALL

Umpire John Sullivan got taken out by a sheep during an 1880s game in Waterbury, Connecticut. The sheep was Waterbury's team mascot and it raced onto the field with two loose dogs and jumped into Sullivan, who tumbled to the ground. Four thousand fans chuckled at the animal aggression.

NOT TAKING ANY BULL

The Austin Senators were playing a home Texas League game on July 28, 1888, when a wild bull appeared and rumbled onto the field. Players scattered to all corners of the ballpark and fans shrieked with fear. When the bull charged at two Austin outfielders, team management decided to stop the game.

FETCH

Olean was battling Bradford in an 1890 New York-Pennsylvania League game when a dog ran onto the field and snatched the baseball. The dog took off and nobody could retrieve the ball. The umpire suspended the game "on account of dog."

BUTTERFLY WINGS

One of the reasons 1890s minor league outfielder Bill Armour never reached the majors was his consuming fear of butterflies.

BLOWIN' IN THE WIND

Employees worked hard to build new bleachers for the Southern Association's Montgomery Senators in 1907. A severe windstorm destroyed the new bleachers a few weeks later.

HIGH VOLTAGE

Lightning struck the Class B Williamsport Millionaires' grandstand on June 24, 1907, setting the stands on fire. The burning bleachers halted that day's game in the fourth inning.

NIGHT LIGHT

Evening baseball was unheard of in 1907, yet the Class D Western Canada League started every game after 6 p.m. that year. Late sunsets in Calgary, Edmonton, Lethbridge, and Medicine Hat, Alberta, made night games possible. The circuit was nicknamed the "Twilight League."

OFF ITS LEASH

A 2015 Triple-A game in El Paso, Texas, was delayed for a few minutes when a wiener dog got loose from a between-innings race and scampered around the field, avoiding players who were trying to pick it up.

MONKEYING AROUND

A chimp's escape turned a Southern Association game into pandemonium on July 17, 1909. "Henry the Chimpanzee," the Class A New Orleans Pelicans' mascot, busted from his cage and chased players around the field. The game was delayed for a few minutes while Henry was restrained.

GET OFF YOUR HIGH HORSE

In 1908, a foul ball soared out of a Class A Providence Grays game and hit a police officer, knocking the cop off his horse.

BURNOUT

Bridgeport and Springfield sweltered for 12 innings on July 11, 1911, in Springfield, Massachusetts, before the umpire ended the Class B game "because of intense heat" and declared it a tie. The July 1911 heat wave sent temperatures as high as 106°F in Massachusetts and heat stroke killed hundreds of New Englanders that month.

THE FILLYS

Newark Indians pitcher Al Schacht rode a horse to the pitcher's mound before a 1914 game in Newark, New Jersey. Schacht met the horse's owner earlier in the day, gave him three dollars and a ticket to the game as a rental fee, and then secured the horse under the bleachers. Once Schacht was announced before the first inning, he hopped on the horse and galloped to the mound.

PLAY THROUGH

For some reason, the Milwaukee Brewers home game on April 20, 1920, wasn't postponed. It was 32°F and lightly snowing at first pitch, and the snowflakes thickened as the innings moved along. By the end of Milwaukee's 15-14 win, there was four inches of snow on the ground and the first baseman couldn't find first base.

ON-BRAND

MLB commissioner Kenesaw Mountain Landis rode a live bull on the field at the Class C Durham Bulls' ballpark opening event in 1926.

DOG BITES

Infielder Karl Swanson and his terrier, Rusty, were traded from the Class D Mississippi Valley League's Moline Plowboys to the Rock Island Islanders in 1928. Rusty became Rock Island's mascot.

THERE'S A SONGBIRD WHO SINGS

In 1931, Chattanooga Lookouts president Joe Engel hung 50 bird cages around his ballpark in Chattanooga, Tennessee, because he liked hearing the birds sing during games.

ELEPHANT IN THE ROOM

Engel's 34-year stint running the Lookouts was filled with loony publicity. He had a duck lay an egg on second base, had players enter the ballpark riding elephants, and had his broadcaster host a pregame show while riding a camel.

WHALE OF A REASON

A 1920s Class D game in North Carolina got beached by a whale. The Wilmington Pirates were playing one afternoon when a fan arrived screaming about a beached whale near the waterfront ballpark. Everyone at the game, including the players, took off for the shore to see the whale. Standing by himself at home plate, umpire Art Knowles postponed the game.

AN APPROPRIATE GIFT

The Class B Dayton Ducks presented manager Ducky Holmes with pet ducks on opening day in 1932. Holmes kept the birds in a pen behind the grandstand.

ANIMAL CONTROL

The Class D Tucson Lizards were warming up between innings of an Arizona-Texas League game in 1932 when a Lizards outfielder ran from the field into the dugout, grabbed a bat, ran back onto the field, and whacked a live rattlesnake that was slithering through the outfield.

WATERLOGGED

One day in the late 1930s, the Class D Williamston Martins' equipment bags fell in a creek outside the ballpark in Snow Hill, North Carolina. Volunteers helped the team wade into the water to rescue the balls and bats. That day's game was delayed while the equipment dried.

RIBBIT

Umpire Donald Atkinson was the victim of a slimy prank during a 1940s Class D game in Georgia. An Albany Cardinals batter hit a ball out of play, so Atkinson reached into his ball bag for a new baseball. He grabbed a live frog instead and was so startled that he tossed the reptile across the field. Atkinson never found out who hid a frog in his ball bag.

WHAT A HOOT

A ball went up and an owl came down during a Class D Kentucky-Illinois-Tennessee League game in Paducah, Kentucky, decades ago. It was a foggy night and an infield pop-up flew into the air. The ball ricocheted into the stands as an owl fell to the field.

CHICKEN COOP

In 1946, a New Hampshire farmer gave live chicks to Class B Nashua Dodgers players after they hit a home run.

DELAWARE ZOO

A monkey attended a Class D Dover Phillies game in Dover, Delaware, on August 19, 1946, and frolicked on a concrete railing behind home plate for the first three innings.

HEDGING YOUR BETS

Hedges were added to fair territory at Atlanta's Spiller Field in 1949. If a fielder caught a ball in a hedge, it was an out, but if a fielder ran through a hedge pursuing a fly ball, the batter was given a home run.

SHOCKED

Jim Martin showed he was the toughest catcher in the Class C West Texas-New Mexico League. The Pampa Oilers' catcher was struck by lightning during the middle of an inning in Abilene, Texas, on April 28, 1950. The force of the lightning bolt catapulted Martin's catcher's mask 20 feet beyond the pitcher's mound. Even though the lightning strike knocked him out, Martin played the next night.

SMUDGE FIRE

One night in 1950, in Gloversville, New York, there was a swarm of mosquitoes in the Class C Gloversville-Johnstown Glovers' bullpen and something had to be done. The annoyed relievers started a fire so the smoke would repel the bugs. But the smoke filled the stadium and the umpires had to delay the game.

BIRDSEED

An easy fly ball hit by Minneapolis batter Bama Rowell turned into a double on June 29, 1950, when a nighthawk pecked the ball out of the air and away from two Milwaukee outfielders. Rowell scored later in the inning and Minneapolis beat Milwaukee that day by one run.

WELL DONE

A steakhouse in Colorado Springs, Colorado, offered a free steak to Class A Colorado Springs Sky Sox players when they hit a home run in 1950. Sky Sox slugger Pat Seerey launched 44 home runs, and at the end of the season, rather than giving him 44 steaks, the restaurant gave him a cow.

HOPS IN HOBBS

The owner of the Class C Hobbs Sports released 12 jackrabbits prior to a game in 1955. The team invited kids onto the field to catch the feisty critters, but they were so fast and jumped so high it was impossible to corral them. The promotion turned into pandemonium. Gates were opened to try and scurry the jackrabbits away. Eventually the game began with three jackrabbits still on the field.

MULE JOCKEY

A Double-A Birmingham player showed agility one night in the 1960s by riding a live mule on the field. He caught a thrown baseball with an empty popcorn box while guiding the mule.

FLOAT ON

A 1969 Double-A Eastern League series between the Elmira Pioneers and Pittsfield Red Sox was so rainy that the nearby Housatonic River flooded and overflowed into left field at Pittsfield's Wahconah Park. Balls hit to deep left field floated away from outfielders, who splashed through the water to retrieve them.

BEWARE OF BEAR

The Triple-A Denver Bears thought of an animalistic way to intimidate opponents in 1970. The Bears acquired a live bear and placed it in a cage in the right field stands.

An uncaged bear walked around on the warning track behind home plate and explored the visitors' dugout at the High-A Asheville Tourists' ballpark on June 8, 2022.

TALES FROM THE DUGOUT

COW TIPPING

Paducah's Walter DeFreitas had to be taken out of the lineup because he was kicked over by a cow. On August 29, 1950, the Class D Paducah Chiefs held a pregame cow-milking contest between DeFreitas and Centralia player Lew Bekeza. DeFreitas lost the milking matchup and the cow added injury to insult, kicking DeFreitas in the leg. The kick was so severe that DeFreitas couldn't play.

WHEN INSECTS ATTACK

A grasshopper invasion postponed the second game of the Double-A Amarillo Giants vs. Midland Cubs doubleheader on August 6, 1972, in Midland, Texas. Thousands of grasshoppers were living behind the center field wall at Midland's Christensen Stadium and when the grounds crew turned on the ballpark's lights for Game 2, the grasshoppers chaotically dispersed. They fluttered around the field and got under fans' clothes. The teams tried to play the game but infielders couldn't see outfielders through the clusters of grasshoppers. The game was postponed, the lights were turned off, and the bugs hopped around town. City officials had to fumigate Midland two days later to get rid of all the grasshoppers.

In more Midland madness, a 1978 Double-A Midland Cubs game was postponed by hundreds of tarantulas that crawled to the field from all over because they were drawn to a new chemical the grounds crew sprayed on the grass.

COLD SEATS

The Double-A Quebec Carnavals had more snow than space after a blizzard in the mid-1970s. They cleared the field, stuffed snow in the stands, and played with fans sitting around the ballpark on snow banks.

BEYOND REPAIR

The Double-A Jersey Indians had to relocate from Jersey City, New Jersey, to Waterbury, Connecticut, in 1979 because a windstorm knocked down a ballpark light tower and Jersey City's government refused to fix it.

FERRET HIM OUT

Hamilton Redbirds infielder Jose Trujillo and his pet ferret were detained one night at the Canadian border in 1989. They were trying to get back to Hamilton, Ontario, but there was an issue with Trujillo's visa.

REEL HIM IN

Ruben Rivera signed a minor league contract with the New York Yankees in 1990 and received $3,070. The $3,000 was a signing bonus and the remaining $70 was repayment for his missed shift working on a fishing boat.

INFESTATION

Six consecutive Triple-A Tidewater Tides games were rained out in 1992 and when the sopping tarp was dragged away, thousands of earthworms were on the field.

SUMMER SNOW SQUALL

It was 88°F in Montana for the Butte Copper Kings' home game on August 21, 1992. One night later, the temperature plummeted to a record low 23°F and Butte's players battled in a baseball blizzard. The game was called in the seventh inning as 2.5 inches of snow fell to the field.

CAUGHT A FISH

The Triple-A Iowa Cubs' ballpark flooded in July 1993 and when the team returned to their wet clubhouse, pitcher Turk Wendell found a fish in his glove.

The I-Cubs should've borrowed an idea from the Class D Chanute Giants in Kansas, who held boat races on their flooded field in 1948.

S'MORES

Half of the independent Lehigh Valley Black Diamonds' roster lived in tents at a Pennsylvania campground during the 2000 season.

MAN VS. HORSE

The Triple-A Rochester Red Wings invited a winless racehorse to try his luck against a human on August 18, 2000. Zippy Chippy brought his 0-86 record to Frontier Field in Rochester, New York, where he raced Red Wings player José Herrera on a makeshift track in the outfield. Herrera won the race and Zippy lost again.

MEOW

The Triple-A Portland Beavers fed 25 feral cats under the grandstands in the early 2000s to help control the stadium's rodent population. Occasionally a few cats emerged behind Portland's bullpen during games.

HEE-HAW

In 2002, Double-A West Tenn Diamond Jaxx pitcher Mark Prior had to wait a few minutes before starting an inning in a Southern League home game because a donkey was slow to get off the field after a between-innings petting zoo promotion.

Five years earlier, also in Tennessee, the Double-A Chattanooga Lookouts had a pregnant donkey named Louise bring baseballs to the umpire during the game.

GAME BIRD

A 2010s High-A California League game in Bakersfield was halted momentarily when a hawk flew into an active electrical line, got electrocuted, and dropped into right-center field.

PURR-FECT PITCH

Bakersfield had a much more positive animal moment on May 20, 2014. A heroic cat named Tara "threw" out the ceremonial first pitch before the Bakersfield Blaze's game that day by pushing the ball with her paw. Tara was invited after a video of her stopping a dog from attacking a boy went viral.

GORILLA RADIO

The Triple-A Omaha Storm Chasers had lines of people waiting for ballpark national anthem auditions in 2011. One hopeful stood out by singing in a gorilla suit.

SWEATY SUIT

St. Paul Saints employee Seigo Masubuchi ran the 2011 Twin Cities Marathon dressed as Mudonna, the team's lovable, furry, pink pig mascot. It was no easy feat; the mascot costume weighed 20 pounds. He ran the full marathon in four hours and five minutes.

In 2022, Masubuchi ran 26.2 miles worth of laps around the concourse during a Saints home game as a fundraiser.

BASEBALL BATS

The Triple-A Oklahoma City RedHawks home game on May 31, 2014, was briefly delayed by bats flying close to the outfielders.

CRABBY

The independent Southern Maryland Blue Crabs scheduled a crab giveaway but got pinched by protests. The club was set to distribute a live crab to the first 1,000 fans on opening day in 2015, but switched to free crab vouchers after objections over the crabs not receiving proper care during the game.

EAGER BEAVER

The Missoula Osprey were three outs from winning a Pioneer League championship in 2015 when a beaver put the celebration on hold. The beaver gnawed at a tree and dropped it onto a power line, shutting down the ballpark's electricity in Missoula, Montana. The Osprey clinched the title after an 18-minute light tower delay.

THE SWAMP

An alligator ran for president in 2016. Canaligator, the Lowell Spinners' mascot, announced his candidacy in January 2016. The campaign had social media pages and an official slogan of "Every night is Opening Night . . . for America."

POSSUM OR OPOSSUM?

The Tennessee Smokies vs. Biloxi Shuckers Double-A Southern League game on April 29, 2016, in Biloxi, Mississippi, was delayed by a possum in the ninth inning. It walked onto the field and Biloxi center fielder Brett Phillips jogged behind it on the warning track until it disappeared behind the fence. The Shuckers gave away Brett Phillips/possum bobbleheads in 2017. The bobblehead shows Phillips stepping toward a possum near his cleats.

MARCEL?

Pitcher Taylor Hawkins had a pet monkey while playing for the Single-A Bowling Green Hot Rods in 2016.

SPOOKY

The Double-A Trenton Thunder's home game on May 13, 2016, in Trenton, New Jersey, had two fog delays that totaled about two hours in length. The foggy Friday was Friday the 13th.

IOWA BUNNIES

There were two different rabbit delays in Iowa in a two-year span. On June 6, 2016, the Triple-A Iowa Cubs' home game against Memphis was halted as a rabbit scampered around the field for two and a half minutes.

One year later, a Single-A Quad Cities River Bandits home game stopped when a rabbit darted around the field on Bark in the Park Day, causing dogs to bark at the rabbit from the stands.

FOXY

In 2016, multiple Single-A Charleston RiverDogs home games were delayed by a fox running around on the field.

HERDING SHEEP

The Batavia Muckdogs vs. State College Spikes New York-Penn League game was delayed by a sheep on August 25, 2016, in State College, Pennsylvania. The Spikes booked Whiplash the Cowboy Monkey to perform between innings and Whiplash's entourage includes a few sheep. One of them wandered onto the field during the game.

HUMP DAY

The Single-A Lansing Lugnuts have had some clever promotions in recent years, like when they brought a live camel named Humphrey to Wednesday home games. Fans took photos with and rode the camel after it delivered first pitch baseballs. The club even put a Humphrey baseball card in its team set.

UNEXPECTED VISITORS

The Single-A Charleston RiverDogs' home game on July 13, 2016, included a raccoon delay. Two raccoons appeared in the third base dugout, scattering players onto the field and into the clubhouse. Grounds crew members captured the raccoons, released them outside the ballpark, and the game resumed after a 10-minute stoppage.

PIGPENS

Parker, the Double-A Richmond Flying Squirrels' rally pig, announced his retirement from baseball in 2016 and moved from the ballpark back to a Virginia farm. Parker made on-field appearances for six seasons and once delayed a game while running down the first base line during an inning.

The Triple-A St. Paul Saints have a new ball pig each year that delivers baseballs and water to the home plate umpire from a satchel on its back.

CATS LOVE DOGS

In 2017, the High-A Lynchburg Hillcats announced dogs were allowed at all of their home games. Dog tickets cost $3 each, with a portion of those sales benefiting the Lynchburg Humane Society.

NIMBLE RODENT

The World's Fastest Squirrel raced at High-A Lake Elsinore Storm games from 2012–2017 in Lake Elsinore, California. The costumed competitor challenged a new fan to a between-innings sprinting showdown at more than 400 games and lost only twice. The dashing mascot was featured on national highlight shows and an ESPN commercial.

BUGABOO

The Triple-A Salt Lake Bees home game on August 5, 2017, was delayed 21 minutes because of bugs fluttering around the ballpark lights. The clusters of bugs were so thick that it blurred the lights and darkened the field.

TOTAL ECLIPSE OF THE START

Salem, Oregon, fell in a solar eclipse's path of totality and the North-west League's Salem-Keizer Volcanoes planned accordingly. The Volcanoes started their home game on August 21, 2017, at 9:45 a.m., then interrupted play when it got dark at 10:15 a.m. It was baseball's first solar eclipse delay and it brought fans from 34 states and eight countries.

GOOSED

A bird delayed the Shorebirds. A goose landed in center field after the second inning of the Single-A Delmarva Shorebirds game in Salisbury, Maryland, on September 2, 2017, and it didn't seem capable of flying away. The start of the third inning was delayed as the goose was assisted by ballpark employees and brought to an animal control facility.

TWO MILLION GALLONS!

Vermont produced more maple syrup than any other U. S. state in 2018 and its professional baseball team introduced a sappy alter-nate identity when the Vermont Lake Monsters became the Vermont Maple Kings for one game that year.

NO PETS ALLOWED

The Double-A San Antonio Missions had a cat-on-the-field delay on May 10, 2018. One night later, there was another delay, and it was less cute. A five-foot-long snake moved through center field until the grounds crew trapped it with a bucket.

GRAB A SLICE

The New York-Penn League's Staten Island Yankees wore Staten Island Pizza Rats uniforms for select games in 2018. The Pizza Rats' name was a nod to a viral video of a rat dragging a full slice of pizza down the steps of a New York City subway station. Staten Island's affiliate, the New York Yankees, were reportedly upset about the pinstripes pizza plan.

SWARMED

The Northwest Arkansas vs. Corpus Christi Double-A game on July 8, 2018, in Corpus Christi, Texas, was delayed an hour and a half because hundreds of bees built a hive on the inside roof of the home dugout. A local beekeeper came out, moved the hive, and the game started.

RENO'S REEK

The Triple-A Reno Aces were batting in the ninth inning on July 16, 2018, in Reno, Nevada, when a skunk crept through a grounds crew gate and wandered around the field for a few minutes, delaying the game.

IN HOT WATER

The Single-A Charleston RiverDogs changed their name and branding for one game in 2018 and morphed into the Charleston Boiled Peanuts. The transformation honored "Tony the Peanut Man," their beloved ballpark peanut vendor who passed away in 2016.

BIRD MAN

Pitcher Jesus Cruz was walking off the field for the Single-A Peoria Chiefs on July 4, 2018, in Peoria, Illinois, when a bird flew into him and fluttered to the ground. Cruz picked up the bird carefully with his glove and put it on top of his head as he walked to the dugout.

VERY LONG JOHN SILVER'S

The Single-A Charleston RiverDogs began selling foot-long fish sticks at their ballpark restaurant in 2022.

HABOOB

That's a fancy word for a massive dust storm, like the one that suspended the Triple-A game in Las Vegas on August 11, 2018.

JETSTREAM

The High-A Lancaster JetHawks postponed a 2019 home game because of winds exceeding 60 mph.

RIVER CATS' CAT

The Triple-A Sacramento River Cats' home game against Albuquerque on August 19, 2019, was delayed because a cat was walking on the warning track. A Sacramento player walked next to the cat and guided it toward a gate so the game could resume.

DUGOUT SECURITY

The Charlotte Stone Crabs played in the High-A Florida State League from 2009–2019 and occasionally alligators crawled to their ballpark from nearby lakes. One time, players arrived and were startled to find a 10-foot, 800-pound gator under their bench.

HARMFUL PET

The High-A Visalia Rawhide franchise was bit by an alligator. Visalia won 100 games and the California League championship in 1978 and its star player Joe Charboneau had a pet alligator. Shortly after the team clinched the title, Charboneau's gator died in a bathtub and Visalia lost its next 10 championship series appearances. Players wore gator skin-themed uniforms for the 2016 playoffs to try and reverse the curse, but it didn't work. Visalia finally won another title in 2019.

A.Q.I.

A Sacramento River Cats vs. Reno Aces Triple-A series had three consecutive games cancelled or relocated in August 2021 because of poor air quality.

GROUNDHOG DAY

Altoona, Pennsylvania, is only 55 miles from Punxsutawney, Pennsylvania, and the Double-A Altoona Curve gave away a Punxsutawney Phil bobblehead before a game in 2022.

COMING TO LIFE

The Double-A Hartford Yard Goats partnered with a local farm and brought live goats named "Fancy Pants and friends" to every home game in 2021.

Speaking of goats, the Triple-A Gwinnett Braves hosted yoga on the field on June 18, 2017, and the team brought live goats to graze the grass during the yoga session. The yogis took selfies with the goats after.

THEY'RE ALL NUTS

The Single-A Modesto Nuts' mascots are named Al the Almond, Wally the Walnut, and Shelley the Pistachio.

MAN'S BEST FRIEND

Jake the Diamond Dog is a golden retriever that travels the country appearing at minor league ballparks. His tricks include bringing the game ball to the pitcher, fetching towels for umpires, and delivering flowers to fans.

Some teams have their own dogs that retrieve bats that were dropped by hitters, like Finn the Bat Dog of the Triple-A Las Vegas Aviators or Turbo of the High-A Bowling Green Hot Rods.

SANDY THE SEAGULL

That's the name of the High-A Brooklyn Cyclones' mascot, who's named after Brooklyn, New York, native and former Brooklyn Dodgers pitcher Sandy Koufax.

THE BEST OF THE REST

CHERRY BOMBS

New Orleans Pelicans player Abner Powell was fined by the Southern League in 1887 for throwing firecrackers at opposing batters in Charleston, South Carolina.

SKYDIVER

The minor league team in Dayton, Ohio, hired a woman to parachute from a hot air balloon onto the field before a game in the 1890s.

HIT SHARPLY

A Pennsylvania State League game was decided by half a run in 1894. Allentown's Mike Kilroy broke his bat in the eleventh inning of a home game against Pottsville and it was the last available bat. Kilroy reportedly walked to a nearby wood pile, grabbed an axe, brought it to the batter's box, swung at the next pitch, connected, and cut the ball in half. One part of the ball was caught by Pottsville's first baseman, while the other part soared over the fence. The umpire credited Allentown with half of a run for Kilroy's fractured fly.

'CAUSE YOU KNOW I'D WALK A THOUSAND MILES

In 1894, struggling New Orleans Pelicans outfielder Dude Esterbrook gave up on baseball and walked 1,000 miles from Louisiana to Washington, D.C. He met up with former teammates there, borrowed some money, and got his life back together.

HITCHHIKER

Esterbrook's story sounds like Chuck Hinton's. Hinton hitchhiked from North Carolina to Washington, D.C. to attend an open tryout in 1956. The Baltimore Orioles brought him to their ballpark, signed him to a minor league contract, and eight years later he was an MLB All-Star.

FARE CHOICE

Nap Lajoie's parents were mad when he decided to quit his job as a horse-and-buggy taxi driver to sign with the Class B Fall River Indians in 1896. It was a smart career change; Lajoie became a Hall of Famer.

COLLUSION

Player paychecks were based on fan attendance during an 1896 Western League postseason series between Indianapolis and Minneapolis, so participants from both teams quietly agreed to fix the first four games to set up a 2-2 series tie. This agreement guaranteed them more games and more money.

JAILBIRD

Santa Cruz Beachcombers outfielder Mike Donlin was in jail for public drunkenness when he found out the St. Louis Cardinals acquired him in 1899. He posted bail, took a train from California to St. Louis, and started his 12-year major league career.

WHERE'S THE ATM?

Troublemaking Michigan State Leaguers had to carry cash in 1899. Umpires fined unruly players during games and league rules said violators had to pay up immediately. Innings were halted until payments were settled. When a player failed to pay a fine within 20 minutes, his team was given a forfeit loss.

IRRITABLE INNKEEPER

The Class B New England League team in Haverhill, Massachusetts, didn't have clubhouses in the early 1900s, so the team rented a room at a nearby house for players and umpires to change in. One day, an umpire returned to the house after a game and found his clothes all over the street. The landlord was mad about an ejection the ump had issued in that day's game.

BUT WHO'S COUNTING?

Providence and Rochester played an unnecessary extra inning on August 3, 1903, in Rochester, New York. Providence scored a run in the fifth but the daydreaming boy operating the scoreboard forgot to post the tally, so umpire Tom Kelly thought it was 0-0 at the end of nine innings. Midway through the tenth, Kelly listened to shouting fans, recognized the oversight, and named Providence the winner.

Similarly, Akron and Youngstown played only eight innings in a Class C Ohio-Pennsylvania League game on May 6, 1910, because the kid running the scoreboard lost track of innings. By the time the umpire realized the mistake, the teams had gone home.

MEDIA RELATIONS

Buck Thiel assaulted a reporter in 1904 and paid the price. The Class A Des Moines Prohibitionists infielder was arrested and fined $10 for attacking a sportswriter. Thiel was furious with the scribe because he described Des Moines' performance as "rotten, disgusting, unpardonable, intolerable, amateurish, juvenile and incompetent" in the newspaper. Thiel was traded to Omaha soon after.

DEAD MAN WALKING

The *Fresno Republican* should have checked its sources. In 1905, the newspaper reported that a California State League game was cancelled because of the sudden death of Lodi outfielder Fred Schleef. Schleef homered a few weeks later and the same newspaper described it by noting that he was "reported dead a couple of weeks ago."

THEY TOOK HIM IN

The Class C Houston Buffaloes were on a train in 1908 when they found a two-year-old boy that had been abandoned by his mother. The team took care of the boy and welcomed him into the clubhouse and hotels. He moved in with infielder Roy Akin and his wife, Carrie, and they legally adopted him. The boy grew up with them and became a foreman with the Dallas Water Department.

MAKING WAVES

On July 20, 1908, Class C Columbia Gamecocks player J.C. Bender stabbed his manager, Win Clark, while aboard a steamship traveling to their next series. Clark survived and Bender was suspended indefinitely.

ROYAL PAUSE

Class A Eastern League games were postponed on May 20, 1910, for a regal reason. All four games were called off out of respect for King Edward VII's funeral that day.

MILLION-DOLLAR NAME

There was a minor leaguer in the 1910s named Ten Million. It was his real name.

BASEBALL-GATE

Future U. S. president Dwight Eisenhower reportedly played outfield for Junction City in the Class D Central Kansas League in 1911 and used a false name to maintain eligibility for collegiate athletics. Eisenhower's alias "Wilson" was paid by the minor league club a year before Eisenhower joined Army's football team at West Point.

PROPERTY LINE

Indiana reverend E. C. Richardson took the Class D Logansport Whitecaps to court in 1911, claiming they played a game too close to his church on July 9 of that year. The judge threw out the case.

SWAT THE FLY

The fly swatter invention originated at a Class A Western League game between Wichita and Topeka in 1911. Kansas State Board of Health doctor Samuel Crumbine was at the game and heard fans chanting "swat that ball!" It gave him the idea for a "Swat the Fly" campaign, which urged people to stop the spread of typhoid fever by killing transmissible bugs that landed on them.

A schoolteacher in Kansas named Frank White saw the campaign and put together a mock-up swatter using a yardstick and wire screen. When Crumbine saw the prototype, he thought back to the ballgame and called the invention a "fly swatter."

THE HALF-HOUR GAME

On August 30, 1916, Winston-Salem and Asheville finished a nine-inning game in only 31 minutes in Asheville, North Carolina. The Class D teams agreed to rapid speed-up procedures so they could catch an afternoon train. Base runners galloped until they were tagged out, pitchers lobbed the ball over the plate, and fielders dashed to the dugout, sometimes even before the third out was recorded. The 200 spectators were furious, as was Asheville owner L. L. Jenkins, who refunded all fans. It's believed to be the fastest nine-inning game in professional baseball history.

MORE THAN EIGHT MEN OUT

As members of the Chicago White Sox conspired to throw the 1919 World Series, a similar gambling scandal ruined the 1919 Pacific Coast League Championship Series. Vernon Tigers first baseman Babe Borton admitted under oath to bribes that fixed the PCL Championship Series. Borton was banned from baseball two years later.

FILLING

Memphis signed a dentist to play third base in 1923. James "Doc" Prothro was a talented town ball player but refused to join distant minor league teams because he wanted to continue his dentistry work in Tennessee. Memphis was his hometown, so he played for the Class A Chickasaws, and by season's end he was in the majors with Washington.

HEADS UP

In the 1920s, fans in Grafton, North Dakota, developed a tradition of throwing silver dollars at batters after clutch hits.

KEY PLAYER

The Cheyenne Indians rewarded their 1923 team MVP with a new typewriter. Top Pacific Coast League players of this era received better prizes. PCL MVPs were given a gold watch.

MULTITASKER

Future Hall of Famer Casey Stengel's first managing assignment came in Massachusetts in 1925 with Class A Worcester. He was also the team's president and right fielder. After the season, the president resigned, the manager was fired, and the right fielder was released.

THE BAMBINO

Babe Ruth participated in an exhibition game at a minor league park in Wilkes-Barre, Pennsylvania, two days after he played in Game 7 of the 1926 World Series. The game ended after six innings because young fans kept running onto the field to ask Ruth for handshakes and autographs.

OUT ON BAIL

A Class A game in Alabama was delayed until a player was released from jail. On August 27, 1927, Birmingham's Max Rosenfeld was arrested for fighting New Orleans shortstop Ray Gardner. The Barons didn't have enough players without Rosenfeld, so both teams and 20,000 fans waited for two hours until Rosenfeld was freed and then the game continued.

VERY SUPERSTITIOUS

At least one court of law believed baseball curses are real. In 1928, California judge Frank Fogalsong released a judicial order to stop Sacramento Senators fan Frank Nutter from attending any Senators playoff games because he believed Nutter was a jinx to the team. Nutter apparently obeyed the order; he wasn't spotted at Sacramento's championship series loss, a defeat nobody could blame on him.

ROOFTOP RADIO

There was a time when teams resisted live broadcast coverage because they feared fans would listen instead of buying tickets. The Class A Cedar Rapids Raiders' 1930s radio refusal didn't stop rebellious sportscaster Bert Wilson, who broadcasted Raiders games from the roof of a house near the ballpark in Cedar Rapids, Iowa. Wilson later announced Chicago Cubs games from an actual press box.

UNDERVALUED

These days, star players receive millions of dollars for equipment endorsements. In the 1930s, San Francisco Seals player and future Hall of Famer Joe DiMaggio signed a 20-year contract with a bat manufacturer for $250.

POST-MORTEM

A Buffalo, New York, baseball fan got an unexpected guest at his funeral on May 5, 1932. Baltimore's Buzz Arlett drove a home run out of Buffalo's Offerman Stadium that day and the baseball flew through a funeral home's window and rolled right up to the casket of the recently deceased fan.

BREAKFAST OF CHAMPIONS

That famous Wheaties slogan was unveiled at a minor league game in 1933 at Nicollet Park in Minneapolis.

OUT OF STOCK

The Newport vs. Johnson City Class D game in Tennessee ended abruptly in the sixth inning on August 5, 1937, because they ran out of baseballs. The crowd was enraged and a small riot ensued. Dozens of spectators ganged up on a set of bleachers, destroying the benches they were sitting on before the baseball supply dried up.

FIVE-ROUND KNOCKOUT

The Los Angeles Angels' home game against the Portland Beavers on April 16, 1939, was shortened to five innings so stadium employees had time to set up a boxing ring for the heavyweight title fight there the next day between Jack Roper and Joe Louis.

REFERENDUM

Clarksdale, Mississippi's city council voted to postpone Election Day one week in 1940 so it wouldn't conflict with the Class C Clarksdale Red Sox' home opener.

DEATH OF A SALESMAN

Class C Palestine Pals outfielder Charlie Metro got released in 1940 when the team owner found out Metro was working part-time as a Fuller Brush salesman.

CLOWNS

Newspaper writers across the country were amused on May 28, 1940, when they saw a Class B Interstate League update come across the ticker. It said the Reading at Wilmington game in Delaware was postponed "on account of circus."

PACKAGE DEAL

The Brooklyn Dodgers purchased the Class B Reading Brooks franchise for $3,000 in 1941, primarily to get the Brooks' team bus.

SPITTING IMAGE

Spitting on the field is common. Spitting at a sportswriter is a different story. Class D Oil City Oilers outfielder Frederick Shoemaker complained to the official scorer after a 1941 game in Pennsylvania because of an error called against him. Sportswriter Joe Szarfaro witnessed the fuss and called Shoemaker a "crybaby" in a newspaper column the next day. Shoemaker saw the article, raged to the press box, spit tobacco juice in Szarfaro's face, and was later suspended for a year. The 21-year-old Shoemaker never played again.

CUT THE LIGHTS

Towns occasionally went dark for practice blackouts during World War II, where government-ordered electricity shutdowns trained residents for defense procedures, and a 1942 Class A Eastern League game between Springfield and Scranton was delayed a half hour because of a practice blackout.

FREE PRESS

Newspaper photographer Johnny Malone ran into shallow center field and snapped a photo of a close play at second base during an early 1940s Southern Association game in Nashville, Tennessee. The umpire kicked Malone off the field and banished him to the top of the grandstand.

PRANKSTER

The Class B Spartanburg Peaches were batting in the bottom of the ninth with the score tied and the bases loaded on July 11, 1947, in Spartanburg, South Carolina, when someone intentionally turned off the stadium lights. Players and fans went home. Tri-State League president C.M. Llewellyn ordered the participants back to the field to finish the game late at night after turning the lights back on. Nobody ever caught the blackout bandit who turned off the lights.

ROLL OF THE DICE

Al McElreath's 17-year minor league career came to an end in 1947 after he was caught trying to get a Class C Muskogee Reds team-mate to join him in conspiring with gamblers.

BROADCASTER BARTER

In 1948, the minor league Atlanta Crackers and major league Brooklyn Dodgers made baseball's first player-for-broadcaster trade. Brooklyn sent minor league catcher Cliff Dapper to Atlanta, and in return, Crackers broadcaster Ernie Harwell was allowed to leave his Atlanta contract to go broadcast Dodgers games.

BASED ON A TRUE STORY

Crash Davis was a focal character in the 1988 hit movie *Bull Durham*, but there was a real player with that name. The real Crash Davis played 140 major league games for the Philadelphia Athletics in the 1940s and played for the Class C Durham Bulls in 1948.

BULLS ON PARADE

Today's Triple-A Durham Bulls celebrate the movie *Bull Durham* during home games by holding a race between tall mascot costumes of Annie, Crash, and Nuke, the movie's central characters.

BORDER PATROL

The Class C Sunset League game between Reno and Mexicali on May 8, 1948, was postponed when Reno's team bus encountered immigration regulations while entering Mexico. The paperwork process dragged on for so long that the crowded Saturday night game had to be shelved. Thousands of Mexicali fans who were waiting patiently at the ballpark became upset when they were told the game wasn't happening.

SLEEPY

The Del Rio Cowboys were too tired to play, so they didn't. On June 20, 1948, the Cowboys' game against the Vernon Dusters was postponed and the Class D Longhorn League's official paperwork listed "travel fatigue" as the reason.

CROWDED CLUBHOUSE

The Brooklyn Dodgers had so many minor leaguers at spring training in the late 1940s that some players were given three-digit uniform numbers.

FOUR DIGITS!

The Triple-A Rochester Red Wings can top that. One of their retired jersey numbers is 8,222, representing the number of shareholders that saved the team financially in 1957.

FOUL PLAY

The Class B Hagerstown Owls felt they were losing too many baseballs in 1949, so fans were ordered to return foul balls that flew into the stands in Hagerstown, Maryland. One collector didn't obey the rule and was ejected after stockpiling dozens of foul balls. The same fan strolled back inside the stadium later in the game and a security guard shot at him. The security guard claimed he was only trying to scare the fan. The fan ran for his life, with baseballs bouncing out of his pockets as he sprinted away.

THE SHOW MUST GO ON

The Texas League's Fort Worth Cats' ballpark burned down on May 15, 1949. Despite charred grandstands and scorched dugouts, the Cats played a home game the next day.

HARMONY

A massive brawl involving fans, players, and umpires interrupted the Class C Central Association game between Kewanee and Cedar Rapids on July 24, 1949, in Cedar Rapids, Iowa. Public address announcer Bob Hahn played the national anthem over the speakers and the rumble stopped out of respect for "The Star Spangled Banner."

PEDESTRIAN

There was a cement sidewalk on the left field grass in fair territory at the Class D Welch Miners ballpark in West Virginia in the 1950s.

BICUSPID BONUS

In 1951, the Cleveland Indians bought sets of false teeth for a minor leaguer's parents as part of their agreement to sign him.

LIVING ARRANGEMENTS

The Class B Norfolk Tars had an uncomfortable catcher in the mid-1950s. After crouching for nine innings each day, he slept in his car overnight after games.

FAN APPRECIATION DAY

A fan showed up early to a Class A game in 1954 and ended up playing for the team. Joe Carolan bought a ticket to a Columbus Cardinals game in Columbus, Georgia, and begged team management for a tryout. The 21-year-old put on a show, hitting line drives all over the field during pregame batting practice. The Cardinals signed him an hour before the game and put him in the lineup. Carolan smashed a grand slam in his first at bat. South Atlantic League pitchers eventually realized Carolan couldn't hit a curveball and the fan-turned-phenom lasted only 33 games with Columbus.

LUCKY CIGAR

When future Hall of Famer Billy Williams signed a minor league contract with the Chicago Cubs in 1956, the deal included $150 a month in salary, $2.25 a day in meal money, and a 15-cent cigar for his dad.

LEGENDARY NEWSCASTER

Dan Rather used to be a baseball broadcaster. He was the radio voice of the Triple-A Houston Buffs in 1959.

FORTUNATE ACCIDENT

Class B Cedar Rapids infielder Joe Trenary was traveling home to California after the 1961 season when he crashed his car. He returned to Cedar Rapids, Iowa, by bus while his car was being fixed. While Trenary was waiting on the mechanic, MLB's Milwaukee Braves called the Cedar Rapids front office seeking a fill-in player for Triple-A Louisville's playoff series and Trenary was the only player in town. Trenary went to Louisville, hit a playoff home run, and helped them win the American Association championship.

RECKLESS DRIVING

Poor parking skills stopped a Class A Florida State League game on August 8, 1964. A fan arrived late to that night's St. Petersburg vs. Daytona Beach game and backed his car into an electrical pole, causing Daytona Beach's ballpark light tower bulbs to spark and burst mid-game. The game was postponed.

TO BE CONTINUED

Idaho Falls, Idaho, radio listeners were left in suspense partway through night game broadcasts in the 1970s. KUPI-AM radio station faced FCC regulations that ordered them to shut down their signal at 9 p.m. each night, so Idaho Falls Angels broadcaster Jim Garshow signed off with phrases like "Idaho Falls leads Billings 2-1 in the sixth inning. We'll tell you who won on our morning show tomorrow."

THE DRAFT

The Double-A Shreveport Braves postponed two games in May 1970 because eight of their players were away on military duty.

GAME OF CHICKEN

Double-A El Paso Diablos manager Moose Stubing let the San Diego Chicken mascot coach third base during a game in the late 1970s. The Famous Chicken got booed off the field when he sent a runner home who got thrown out by 20 feet.

MILKMAN

The Double-A Macon Peaches couldn't afford new base-balls for batting practice in the early 1960s, so manager Dave Bristol washed the dirty baseballs with milk to keep them white.

ALTERNATE IDENTITY

A man changed his name and scammed the San Diego Padres into a minor league contract in 1974. Meat butcher Rich Pohle felt as athletic as he was two decades before, when he was a teenage baseball standout. He knew teams would never sign a 36-year-old, so he arrived at a Padres tryout disguised as 21-year-old Australian infielder "Rocky Perone." Pohle wore a wig, applied youthful facial cream, and faked an Australian accent. The Padres liked his skills, believed his act, signed him, and sent him to the Northwest League's Walla Walla Padres. Pohle's scam lasted only one game. An opposing manager recognized him from a tryout 12 years before and reported him. Pohle came clean and was released.

ANGRY GUY

Single-A Lodi Dodgers reliever Guy Todd detonated in 1976. He hadn't pitched in a week and was furious at the Los Angeles Dodgers organization. So when his manager told someone else to warm up one night, Todd ripped off his jersey, threw it over the wall, stormed across the field during an inning, left the ballpark, and retired.

IT VANISHED

A fly ball disappeared from a Double-A game on May 28, 1978. The Double-A Jersey Indians were batting against the Bristol Red Sox in the early innings at Roosevelt Stadium in Jersey City, New Jersey, when an Indians batter lifted a fly ball to right field and the ball disappeared! Nobody on the field, in the stands, or in the bullpens could determine where the ball went. The umpires got together and gave the batter a double.

MUSICAL CHAIRS

A batboy was ejected from a Triple-A game in Oregon. Sam Morris, the 14-year-old Portland Beavers batboy, watched from the on-deck circle as Portland manager Lee Elia was thrown out of the game on May 27, 1984. During his tirade, Elia grabbed a chair and threw it on the field. Elia went to the clubhouse, but the chair was still resting on the infield turf, and umpire Pam Postema wouldn't clean up after the ejected manager. She demanded Morris pick up the chair, but the batboy refused, so Postema ejected him too.

LOSE YOUR HEAD

In 1984, Jose Canseco and two Single-A Modesto A's teammates stole the Bakersfield Dodgers' mascot costume's head after a game in Bakersfield, California. Canseco brought Roger the Dodger's head onto the team bus and transported it all the way back to Modesto. It wasn't returned to Bakersfield until the following season.

CREAMED

Two people got ejected from the Double-A El Paso Diablos' game on May 24, 1988, and neither one of them were on the field. First, public address announcer Paul Strelzin got tossed for playing the song "When Will I Be Loved?" after an argued call at home plate. As the announcer was being escorted from the booth, a resentful fan threw an ice cream at an umpire and got tossed too.

OH SNAPP

Wilbur Snapp, the Single-A Clearwater Phillies' organist, was ejected from a game in 1985 for playing "Three Blind Mice" after a call against Clearwater.

BE KIND, REWIND

Three members of the 1989 Bellingham Mariners couldn't find an affordable apartment in Bellingham, Washington, so they brought sleeping bags into an abandoned video store and lived there.

DOES IT HURT WHEN YOU SLEEP?

Triple-A Buffalo infielder Chris Brown missed a game in 1989 because of a sore eyelid. He told his manager he slept on it wrong.

UNIFORMITY

Carlos Quintana wore his Red Sox uniform for two different teams on June 2, 1989. In the first inning of the Triple-A Pawtucket Red Sox' 6 p.m. home game, MLB's Boston Red Sox summoned Quintana for their home game at 7:30 p.m. He raced out of Pawtucket's McCoy Stadium in uniform and hopped into a running car waiting for him. Dropped off at Boston's Fenway Park minutes before game time after a 50-mile drive, Quintana put on a Boston cap and joined the major league team. The Red Sox and PawSox had the same home uniforms.

INCIDENTALS

The Quad City Angels learned not to cross hotel owners in the Midwest League. The Single-A club bickered for a year with The Works Hotel in South Bend, Indiana, about a bill. The Angels made reservations for a series in 1988 but decided to stay somewhere else and the hotel threatened legal action if they didn't pay up. On July 11, 1989, a South Bend sheriff entered the Quad City clubhouse and took jerseys, bats, and helmets after a court decision saying police could seize the equipment until the bill was paid. The parent California Angels wired money to the hotel in time for Quad City's next game.

FELONS ON THE FIELD

The Single-A Beloit Snappers needed extra bodies on rainy nights to pull the tarp in the 1990s, so they set up an arrangement with a local jail. Whenever rain was forecasted, a van full of eager inmates arrived and assisted the grounds crew. Sometimes the prisoners even stuck around for the game.

SUMMER HOCKEY

Vancouver, British Columbia's Nat Bailey Stadium is cozy and doesn't have photographers' platforms behind the outfield fence, so when a local television station aired Triple-A games from there in the 1990s, a photographer shot the action from the warning track. Fearful of being hit by a baseball or an outfielder, the cameraman wore a hockey helmet.

RSVP

Greenville Braves prospect and future Hall of Famer Chipper Jones missed the 1992 Double-A Southern League Championship Series because the games conflicted with his wedding.

MOONING

The Double-A Memphis Chicks' mascot was thrown out of a game in 1993 for turning his back to an umpire and pulling up his loin cloth garment.

ON THEIR RADAR

The FCC fined the Triple-A Norfolk Tides $8,000 in 1993 for using an unlicensed radar gun at their ballpark.

NAME RECOGNITION

The High-A California League's High Desert Mavericks had two broadcasters named Dave Schultz in 1993. One was the lead voice and the other filled in on some road games.

PHANTOM OF THE BALLPARK

In the 1990s, the High-A Fort Myers Miracle had a Phantom of the Opera–like character who appeared on the field shooting sparks during between-innings skits. One night, the Phantom fell while climbing onto the field and accidentally pressed his sparks button, lighting his cape on fire.

DON'T TRY THIS AT HOME

The Single-A Kane County Cougars had to delay a game in 1993 because their field caught on fire. A touring performer named "Jymmy the Villain" planned to dramatically run around the field between innings, climb onto a trampoline, and bounce over flaming blocks of wood. But while Jymmy was prancing around, the boards became too hot for his assistants to handle. They dropped the burning wood and ignited the grass. The game was halted while the field fire was extinguished.

INVESTIGATIVE REPORTING

The Single-A Lansing Lugnuts hadn't yet announced their team name when they discreetly set up their merchandise store "Nuts and Bolts" in 1995. The night before the team name announcement, a newspaper reporter found a gap in the screen covering the store's wall, looked inside, identified the moniker, and broke the news before the team did.

WHO WASHED THE UNIFORMS?

Beloit Snappers clubhouse manager Jason DeZwarte was thrown out of a Single-A Midwest League game in Kane County, Illinois, in 1996 for arguing balls and strikes from the dugout.

HOLY WATER

A Triple-A Calgary Cannons home game was delayed in 1997 because the ballpark sprinklers came on and the grounds crew couldn't shut them off. A priest appeared from the stands with a bucket, placed it over one of the sprinklers, and sat on the bucket to contain the water.

There were no priests available on August 3, 2021, in Eastlake, Ohio, when the sprinklers accidentally turned on and sprayed players while Micah Pries of the Single-A Lake County Captains trotted around the bases after a home run.

WELL, HAIR PRODUCTS ARE FLAMMABLE

Little Rock, Arkansas, police spotted a suspicious truck outside a Double-A Arkansas Travelers home game on July 31, 1998. The cops called in the bomb squad and considered evacuating fans from the ballpark. Travelers front office members saw the commotion and explained the truck was there to deliver hair products for a post-game fan giveaway.

OFF-BASE

A Double-A Texas League game was suspended because of a busted base. Wichita's Carlos Febles slid hard into second in Midland, Texas, on August 1, 1998, and the base broke from its stem. The grounds crew tried repairing the base, then unsuccessfully tried pushing a home plate into the second base slot. The managers believed the unsteady base was a safety hazard to players, so the game was suspended in the seventh inning.

BYE-CLAWS

Single-A Lakewood BlueClaws groundskeeper Bill Butler was ejected from a game on May 23, 2003, in Lakewood, New Jersey. Butler and both clubs' managers wanted the field to be tarped because of mid-game rain, but that's the umpires' decision, and the umps wanted the game to continue. When the two umpires got together to discuss the situation, Butler walked onto the field holding a local radar map, hoping to join the conversation. He was told to get off the field and was thrown out of the game.

OOPS! I WORE IT AGAIN

The Double-A Birmingham Barons had Britney Spears to thank when their cap sales spiked in 2004. The world-famous entertainer wore a Barons cap in the music video for her hit song "Everytime." The Barons wondered why she picked their cap, they even contacted Spears' publicist, but they didn't get a reply.

HE NEEDS A BIGGER GARAGE

Larry Trujillo is the luckiest baseball fan in New Mexico. On August 1, 2005, he entered a contest at a Triple-A Albuquerque Isotopes game, his name was drawn, and Albuquerque's Jason Wood hit a grand slam to win Trujillo a new car. Trujillo entered the same contest on May 5, 2006, and Albuquerque's Paul Hoover also hit a grand slam, winning Trujillo his second new car in a nine-month span.

BENEFITS

Mike Mordecai was a major league player and a minor league manager in the same season. Mordecai managed the New York-Penn League's Jamestown Jammers in 2005. His playing career ended a few days shy of accruing 10 years of MLB service time, so Jamestown's parent club, the Florida Marlins, activated him as a player after Jamestown's season ended so he would have enough service time to receive the full players' pension. Mordecai got into two Marlins games that September.

TEAM CHEMISTRY

The Triple-A Omaha Royals were in the fourth inning of their home game on May 28, 2008, when Rosenblatt Stadium had to be evacuated because a nearby train leaked 200 gallons of hydrochloric acid.

BUNT STUNTS

The Single-A Clinton LumberKings made bunts exciting. The LumberKings held a skills contest and home run derby the night before the 2009 Midwest League All-Star Game. The skills competition included a sudden-death bunt-off. Fans cheered like a golf crowd witnessing a dramatic putt when Dee Gordon's bunt wandered into the "three-point circle" to win the bunt-off.

MISMATCH

The Single-A Beloit Snappers' roster had base-ball's tallest and shortest player in 2008. Seven-foot-1 pitcher Loek Van Mil towered over 5-foot-3 infielder Chris Cates. The teammates were separated by 22 inches.

PARTING GIFTS

Elaine Fulps defeated other Grand Prairie AirHogs fans in the "Pallbearers Race" and "Mummy Wrap" on-field contests on June 3, 2008, to earn a free casket, funeral, and headstone from a local funeral home when she passes away.

FATHER'S DAY

When the Single-A Lansing Lugnuts' manager Sal Fasano missed a game vs. Clinton on July 24, 2010, his hitting coach John Tamargo Jr. took over. The visiting LumberKings were managed by Tamargo's father, John Tamargo Sr. The son's team won 12-7.

On July 7, 2015, father and son Ronnie Whiting and Ronnie Whiting Jr. were the only two umpires on the field for Stephen Tarpley's no-hitter for the Single-A West Virginia Power in Charleston, West Virginia.

IN DA CHUKARS CLUB

Hip-hop artist 50 Cent donned an Idaho Falls Chukars cap in the music video for his 2011 single "Wait Until Tonight." It was a random and unexpected wardrobe choice from the New York-born rap superstar. The Chukars later invited 50 to perform the national anthem at Melaleuca Field in Idaho. They're still waiting for a reply.

TASTE THE RAINBOW

It was raining candy in California on May 22, 2011. The High-A Visalia Rawhide hired a helicopter to hover over the field and drop 700 pounds of candy after a game. Herds of kids were restrained behind a rope, drooling at the thought of free candy. After the sweets splashed to the grass, the children were unleashed and the candy free-for-all ensued.

AREA 51

If you canvassed the Triple-A Pacific Coast League standings on July 24, 2011, you may have thought you were seeing triple. The Las Vegas 51s had a 51-51 record.

PERSISTENCE

A Double-A Huntsville Stars fan sat in a car for nine days to win the team's 2011 "Car Survivor" contest. Shawn Harris endured Alabama's summer humidity until the four other contestants bailed, scoring Harris a free 2007 Honda Accord. People were captivated by the captivity, peeking into the crowded car before and after Stars games. Harris was in tears when he gave the car to his mother as a gift.

HEADLESS CRUSHER

Stomper, the independent Lake Erie Crushers' mascot, had to miss a few games when someone stole his head in 2011. The thief returned the head a few days later by inconspicuously placing it under the ballpark's tarp in Avon, Ohio.

HUNGRY ANIMAL

When the Triple-A Rochester Red Wings had George "The Animal" Steele throw out a ceremonial first pitch in 2012, the professional wrestling legend bit into a baseball, chewed off its cover, and flung the mangled ball to the catcher. Steele was famous for chomping on the turnbuckle pads inside the ring during his wrestling days.

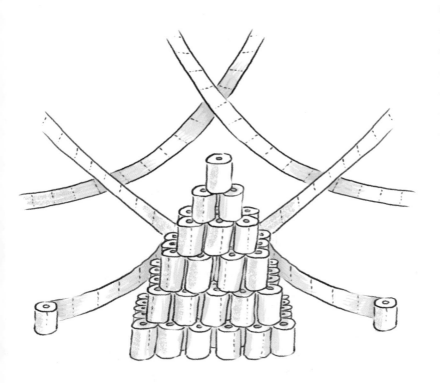

TWO-PLY

The Single-A Wisconsin Timber Rattlers rolled out "Salute to Toilet Paper Night" on August 1, 2012. Appleton, Wisconsin, has a long history of paper production and this theme night included toilet paper streaming from the rafters and a massive toilet paper roll pyramid.

EX-PORT-ED

Stockton Ports fan Will MacNeil was ejected by home plate umpire Mike Huus in the bottom of the fifteenth inning of Stockton's High-A California League home game on May 21, 2013. MacNeil was tossed for yelling at the umpire from the stands after a called strike. The team let MacNeil watch the rest of the game while hiding behind a merchandise stand on the concourse.

WHAT A TANGLED WEBB WE WEAVE

An athletic trainer was thrown out of a game without saying a word on July 24, 2013. Everett trainer Spyder Webb was standing in the dugout with his hands a few inches apart and Northwest League umpire Jeff Gorman interpreted Webb's hand placement as questioning a call at first base, so he tossed him from the game.

HERE COMES THE BRIDE, HERE COMES THE PITCH

The Triple-A Pacific Coast League's first mid-game wedding was completed in 60 seconds. Two Sacramento River Cats fans were married on the field between innings of the River Cats' home game on August 17, 2013. Team mascot Dinger gave away the bride.

UNEXPLAINED

A blue UFO briefly hovered above the right field fence during the Vancouver Canadians' home game on September 3, 2013. The sighting received international media coverage and video analysis from UFO experts, some of whom theorized it was a prank using a kite with lights.

INKED UP

Some Syracuse Chiefs fans displayed permanent passion for their team in 2014. The Triple-A club offered 36 prizes of lifetime season tickets for those willing to get a tattoo showing the team's logo. The spots filled up quickly, but those 36 logo tattoos became outdated five years later when the team changed its name to Syracuse Mets.

CARDIO

Single-A Charleston RiverDogs broadcaster Sean Houston called an entire game from the concourse while walking on a treadmill on June 19, 2014. His sweaty show was part of a promotion for a local treadmill retailer.

MORE TREADMILL TALK

The San Diego Padres traded minor league catcher Sean Mulligan to Cleveland for $75,000 and a used treadmill in 1997.

GET CHECKED

High-A Myrtle Beach Pelicans general manager Andy Milovich received a prostate exam while singing "Take Me Out to the Ballgame" during the seventh-inning stretch of his team's home game on July 24, 2014. He was in a booth with a doctor while the videoboard camera showed him from the neck up.

EXTRA CHEESE

The High-A Carolina Mudcats had a pizza delivered to the dugout during a 2014 road game in Myrtle Beach, South Carolina.

DUMBBELL

A Tri-City ValleyCats strength and conditioning coach was ejected from the decisive third game of the New York-Penn League Championship Series on September 9, 2014.

AUTHORITATIVE VOICE

South Bend Cubs public address announcer Jon Thompson moved from the press box to the field on May 11, 2015, to umpire a Single-A game in South Bend, Indiana. Thompson was a longtime high school umpire and was asked to fill in because a regularly scheduled umpire was hit by a foul ball and suffered a concussion.

BAZAAR DELAY

The High-A Tampa Yankees' home game on August 7, 2015, was postponed because of flashing lights from a circus tent behind the center field fence. The lights would've distracted hitters.

SIRENS

The Double-A New Britain Rock Cats had a fire department park one of its trucks in left field for a pregame ceremony on August 28, 2015. The truck sank into the grass and didn't budge out of its hole until an hour later, leaving behind a divot and a delay.

IMPERSONATION

Joe Gillespie was on probation in 2016 after a memorable larceny arrest. Gillespie passed out after drinking at an event in the Triple-A Charlotte Knights' ballpark, woke up at 12:30 a.m. alone in the stadium, opened the mascot's locker room, put on the mascot costume, walked out of the stadium, and bar-hopped in Charlotte, North Carolina, dressed as the mascot Homer until 5 a.m. The police knocked on Gillespie's door the next morning, saw Homer's head on a couch, and arrested him.

ARACHNOPHOBIA

High-A Stockton Ports coaches and players stood up and moved to the top of the dugout during a 2016 road game in Adelanto, California, because the back of the dugout was full of black widow spiders.

TWO DRAWS

There hadn't been a Triple-A Pacific Coast League tie in 20 years before May 30, 2016, when two PCL games ended with tie scores. Tacoma and New Orleans were deadlocked 2-2 in the sixth inning when heavy rain made the field unplayable. It was already an official game, and it was the last time the two teams were scheduled to meet, so the game ended in a tie. Later that day, Colorado Springs and Fresno were tied 6-6 in the tenth inning when a travel curfew was reached. It was also the last time those teams were scheduled to meet, so that game ended in a tie also.

DAREDEVILS

Aerialist Nik Wallenda walked across a 500-foot tightrope that was 125 feet above the field before the independent Rockland Boulders' home game in New York on June 25, 2016. Nik's great-grandfather Karl Wallenda performed a similar stunt before a 1976 Triple-A Rochester Red Wings home game at age 71. Neither Wallenda had a net below them.

PROBATE

Longtime baseball fan Marion O'Connor died in 2016 and left the Double-A Binghamton Rumble Ponies $195,000 in her will. The team used the unexpected gift on ballpark improvements.

WHO?

The High-A Rancho Cucamonga Quakes game on May 31, 2017, was delayed by a mascot who wasn't even theirs. Eddie the Owl, who was there representing a local credit union, went down with an injury and halted the game for a few minutes in the first inning.

It wasn't baseball's only mascot injury delay. On May 21, 2016, the Triple-A Albuquerque Isotopes employee who was dressed as a jar of salsa hurt their leg during an in-game chile race and had to be helped off the field.

MICAH-LANGELO

Micah Johnson retired from playing after spending the 2018 season with the Triple-A Durham Bulls. He's now a thriving painter with NFT art sales valued at more than $19 million.

BOOMING VOICE

The Triple-A Tacoma Rainiers' home game was halted by a fire alarm on May 22, 2018, and the ballpark's sound system was shut down so it wouldn't interfere with the alarms. When the game continued, public address announcer Randy McNair introduced batters by bellowing their names from the press box, with no microphone.

BUTTER SCULPTURES?

The Triple-A Syracuse Chiefs became the Syracuse Devices for one game in 2018 to honor The Brannock Device Company, which has operated in Syracuse, New York, since the 1920s. One year later, Syracuse played a game as the Syracuse Butter Sculptures, which was an ode to the massive butter sculptures on display at the annual New York State Fair in Syracuse.

BAT MAN

Pensacola's award-winning batboy isn't a boy at all. Terry Williams retrieves the bats and balls at Double-A Pensacola Blue Wahoos home games and was named Southern League Batboy of the Year in 2018 at age 66.

SPORT CLIPS

Baseball writer Ben Hill shaved the head of Double-A Trenton Thunder employee Vince Marcucci between innings of a game in Trenton, New Jersey, on May 18, 2018. The high-speed haircut was part of a Vs. Cancer fundraiser.

LONG DRIVE

Pensacola-area native and Masters champion golfer Bubba Watson is a part-owner of the Double-A Pensacola Blue Wahoos. The team's ballpark restaurant and bar is named Bubba's Sand Trap.

BURN NOTICE

Uncle Slam was the High-A Potomac Nationals' mascot from 2005–2019. He appeared at most games during that time, with the exception of a 60-day stint on the injured list when his costume was burned in a fire.

HANG TIGHT

On July 13, 2019, the Double-A Akron RubberDucks home game paused 15 minutes in the eighth inning because a city festival's fireworks show was distracting batters.

DRINK UP

The Triple-A El Paso Chihuahuas have transformed into the El Paso Margaritas for select games every year since 2019. The margarita was reportedly invented in the El Paso, Texas/Juarez, Mexico, region in 1942.

NOT OVER 'TIL IT'S OVER

On August 14, 2019, in Lancaster, California, the High-A Lake Elsinore Storm trailed the Lancaster JetHawks 13-3 with two outs in the ninth inning and a runner at first base. The Storm then scored 10 runs in the ninth and one run in the tenth to win 14-13.

PLUGGING HOLES

Five years after an unexpected sinkhole swallowed eight cars under the National Corvette Museum in Bowling Green, Kentucky, the Single-A Bowling Green Hot Rods played a game as the Bowling Green Sinkholes on August 30, 2019.

HEISMAN TROPHY WINNER

Former NFL quarterback Tim Tebow played in the New York Mets' minor league system from 2016–2019. He batted .222 in 306 games and reached Triple-A before retiring from baseball.

CAMPAIGN SEASON

Two different teams temporarily rebranded to recognize their states' early roles in the U. S. presidential primary process. In 2020, the Double-A New Hampshire Fisher Cats revealed plans to become the New Hampshire Primaries for one game, while the Triple-A Iowa Cubs played a game as the Iowa Caucuses in 2019.

KNIGHT IN SHINING ARMOR

The Triple-A Charlotte Knights' mascot Homer helped put out a fire on March 9, 2021. Homer, who is ironically a fire-breathing dragon, was in the middle of a ballpark photo shoot when he noticed a fire in a park across the street. He grabbed a ballpark fire extinguisher, ran across the street, and put out the fire before the fire department arrived.

STAY AT HOME

At least one young man in Jackson, Tennessee, wasn't quarantining on April 26, 2020. The unknown trespasser was bored, so he broke into the Double-A Jackson Generals' ballpark and used team equipment to record a positive, encouraging video on a press box computer. He didn't steal or damage anything.

FALSE ALARM

Single-A Jupiter's Cameron Barstad hit a foul ball out of play to the third base side on June 18, 2021, in Jupiter, Florida. The ball hit a fire alarm and broke it, activating all fire alarms throughout the ballpark. The fans evacuated and returned when they were told there was no fire.

THE JERK STORE CALLED

George Costanza was famously told "The ocean called, they're running out of shrimp" in a *Seinfeld* episode. On July 10, 2021, the Triple-A Jacksonville Jumbo Shrimp gave away 2,000 bobbleheads showing Costanza with an open mouth, feasting on a plate of shrimp.

RENEGADE ANNOUNCER

On August 11, 2021, the High-A Hudson Valley Renegades gave out a bobblehead of their public address announcer, Rick Zolzer, to commemorate the time he was ejected for announcing that the umpires "were clowns that could only get to a big league game by buying a ticket." Zolzer is a character who once announced a game via Skype from his pool, a gimmick the team called "Zolz on Deck."

DRONE ON

The Columbus vs. Memphis Triple-A game on August 24, 2021, in Memphis, Tennessee, was halted for a few minutes because a drone was hovering over the field.

High-A Rancho Cucamonga catcher Connor Wong tried to end a drone delay quickly in Lancaster, California, on August 30, 2018. The flying device was lingering above the field when Wong wound up and threw a ball at it. He missed.

WHO LIVES IN A PINEAPPLE UNDER THE SEA?

When eight-time MLB All-Star Robinson Canó signed a Triple-A contract with the San Diego Padres on June 10, 2022, he got a quick reminder that he was back in the fun-loving minor leagues. In his first game with the El Paso Chihuahuas, the team wore SpongeBob SquarePants jerseys that were auctioned off for charity after the game.

ASSORTMENT

Some minor league teams sell 70 or more different caps featuring their team logos.

NOSEY

Johnny Doskow has called Triple-A Sacramento River Cats games since 2001 and is known for his big voice and his big beak. The team once honored Doskow and his nose by giving out "Johnny Doskow Bobblenose" bobbleheads to fans.

STATE CAPITAL

The River Cats hold a between-innings "Heads of State" race featuring big-headed costumes of former California governors Gray Davis, Ronald Reagan, and Arnold Schwarzenegger.

BIG-TIME BATBOYS

Major leaguers Cameron Maybin and Cal Ripken Jr., author Thomas Wolfe, and NCAA basketball coach Roy Williams all spent part of their childhoods as Asheville Tourists batboys in North Carolina.

BALLPARK BUZZ

The Double-A Rocket City Trash Pandas have a mobile barbershop set up on the left field concourse. Haircuts are available to all fans during every game. As for that team name, Rocket City is a nickname for Huntsville, Alabama, where there's a NASA Space Flight Center. "Trash panda" is a slang term for a raccoon.

TURN OUT THE LIGHTS

The High-A Asheville Tourists and Single-A Columbia Fireflies both have logos on their caps that glow in the dark.

HAUNTED HOTEL

Some International League players have switched hotels in Scranton, Pennsylvania, after being spooked by paranormal activity at their original hotel. The Radisson Lackawanna Station Hotel was converted from a historic train station and it's rumored to be haunted. One player left after seeing a ghoulish man in a tuxedo, and another had a similar encounter with a phantom boy wearing a San Francisco Giants cap.

RICHTER SCALE

The Single-A Rancho Cucamonga Quakes' ballpark is nicknamed "The Epicenter" and it sits near multiple earthquake fault lines. The team's mascots are named Tremor and Aftershock.

WAYBACK MACHINE

Once a year, High-A Lansing Lugnuts broadcaster Jesse Goldberg-Strassler leaves his booth and recreates a game broadcast from elsewhere, like sportscasters did a century ago when they didn't travel. Goldberg-Strassler receives pitch-by-pitch info via instant messenger, invents elaborate descriptions based on those brief messages, and uses baseball sounds and pre-recorded crowd noise to mimic ballpark atmosphere.

DANCING DIRT DUDES

That's the name of the Triple-A Lehigh Valley IronPigs grounds crew/dance troupe that performs while dragging the infield between innings.

FIRST ROBOT UMPIRES, NOW THIS

The Triple-A Louisville Bats started using a robotic mower to cut their field in 2022. The grounds crew programs the new device with a handheld scheduler.

GOOD MECHANICS

Speaking of robots, a group of high school students built one and programmed it to throw out the ceremonial first pitch before the Lowell Spinners' home game in Massachusetts, on August 20, 2016.

HIDDEN TREASURE

The High-A Spokane Indians' office contains a rusty, vintage safe that was discovered during ballpark renovations. Some have speculated the safe is more than 65 years old. Despite curiosity about its contents, the team keeps the safe unopened so its mystery will endure.

90s NIGHTS

The actors who played Mr. Belding on *Saved by the Bell*, Al Borland on *Home Improvement*, and The Soup Nazi on *Seinfeld* are among the celebrities who make appearances at minor league ballparks.

ACKNOWLEDGEMENTS

I hoped for a visual book of minor league stories with fun illustrations, and there's no publisher that would execute that plan better than Cider Mill Press. Thank you to founder and publisher John Whalen, his staff, and designer Ben Sampson. Their vision and artwork made this book a success.

This book includes stories about Buzz Arlett, Buzz Clarkson, and Buzz Laird, and I'd like to thank another Buzz—editor Buzz Poole, who had great enthusiasm for this project from the beginning.

I'd also like to thank my family, especially Heather and Carson, and all of the great baseball fans in El Paso, Texas.

ABOUT THE AUTHOR

Tim Hagerty is the broadcaster for the Triple-A El Paso Chihuahuas and has called professional baseball games since 2004. His baseball history articles have appeared in *Baseball Digest*, *MLB.com*, *Sporting News*, *The Hardball Times*, and other publications.

This is his second book. His first, *Root for the Home Team: Minor League Baseball's Most Off-the-Wall Team Names and the Stories Behind Them*, was published by Cider Mill Press in 2012.

SOURCES

100 Things A's Fans Should Know & Do Before They Die, 1957 San Francisco Seals: End of an Era in the Pacific Coast League, ABC15 Arizona, *Abilene Reporter-News, A Game of Inches, Akron Beacon Journal,* Alan Ledford, *Albuquerque Journal,* Alex Freedman, Alex Herrnberger, *Always on Sunday: The California Baseball League, 1886 to 1915, Amarillo-Globe Times,* American Association, Andrew Green, *Antelope Valley Press,* Anthony Rifenburg, *Arizona Daily Star, Arizona Republic, Arkansas Baseball, Arkansas Democrat-Gazette,* Arthur O. Schott, *Asbury Park Press, Asheville Citizen, Asheville Citizen-Times,* Associated Press, *Atlanta Constitution, At the Yard Magazine, Austin American-Statesman, Bakersfield Californian, Ballpark Digest, Baltimore Sun, Baseball America, Baseball Digest, Baseball Dope for 1909, Baseball from Browns to Diablos, Baseball Guide from the Office of the Baseball Commissioner, Baseball in Baltimore: The First Hundred Years, Baseball in Minnesota: The Definitive History, Baseball in Mobile, Baseball Legends and Lore, Baseball Library, Baseball on the Prairie, Baseball: Past and Present, Baseball Pilgrimages, Baseball-Reference.com, Baseball's Book of Firsts, Baseball's Canadian-American League, Baseball's Hall of Fame: Where the Legends Live Forever, Baseball's Hometown Teams: The Story of the Minor Leagues, Baseball's Longest Games: A Comprehensive Worldwide Record Book, Battered Bastards of Baseball, Beating the Bushes,* Ben Hill, *Billings Gazette,* Biloxi Shuckers, *Birmingham News, Birmingham Post-Herald, Bismarck Tribune,* BlueRidgeLeague.org, Boise Hawks, *Boston Globe, Bourbon News,* Bowie Baysox, Bradenton Marauders, Brad Taylor, Branch Rickey III, *Brew Crew Ball, Bricks and Bats: Professional Baseball: Lowell, Massachusetts, Bridgeport Herald, Bridgeport Times and Evening Farmer,* Brockton Rox, *Brooklyn Daily Eagle,* Brotherhood of Locomotive Engineers and Trainmen, *Buffalo Commercial, Burlington Free Press,* Burl Yarbrough, *Bush League – A History of Minor League Baseball, Bush League Boys: The Postwar Legends of Baseball in the American Southwest, California Baseball: From the Pioneers to the Glory Years, Capital Times, Carlsbad Current-Argus,* CBS Sports, Charleston RiverDogs, *Char-*

lotte Observer, *Chattanooga Daily Times, Chattanooga News, Chicago Tribune,* Chris Hagstrom-Jones, Chris Schleicher, Chuck Greenberg, Chuck McGill, *Clarion-Ledger, Class C Baseball, A Case Study of the Schenectady Blue Jays in the Canadian-American League, 1946-1950,* Clinton LumberKings, *Clowning Through Baseball, Colorado Springs Gazette,* Colorado Springs Sky Sox, *Columbia Business Report, Commercial Appeal, Concord Evening Standard,* Corey Hart, *Cornell Daily Sun, Corvallis Gazette-Times, Coshocton Morning Tribune, Creative Loafing Charlotte, Cut4, Daily Arkansas Gazette, Daily Gate City, Daily Herald, Daily Press, Daily News, Daily Tribune, Dallas Morning News, Danville Register & Bee,* Dan Zusman, Darren Headrick, Dave Schultz, David Fleitz, Daytona Cubs, *Dayton, Daily News,* Dennis Holmberg, Derek Sharrer, *Des Moines Register, Detroit Free Press, Diamonds in the Dusk, Doff Your Caps to the Champions – Schenectady,* Donny Baarns, Doug Greenwald, Doug Malan, Durham Bulls, *Eastern Shore League Museum, Elmira Advertiser, El Paso Herald, El Paso Herald-Post, El Paso Times,* Erik Bremer, *ESPN,* Eugene Emeralds, Evan Stockton, *Evening Star, Evening Sun, Everett Herald, Everything Happens in Chillicothe, Facebook, Fall River Daily Evening News, Florida Times-Union, Fort Lauderdale News, Fortune, Fort Wayne Journal-Gazette, Fort Worth Star-Telegram,* Fox 5 DC, Fox 61, Fresno Grizzlies, Gary Jones, *Gazette and Daily, Gazette Extra, Getting in the Game: Inside Baseball's Winter Meetings, Grand Rapids Press,* Great Falls Voyagers, *Green Bay Press-Gazette, Green Cathedrals, Greenville News, Gwinnett Daily Post, Hartford Courant, History of Baseball in California and Pacific Coast Leagues, Honolulu Advertiser,* Hudson Valley Renegades, *Huffington Post, Humor Among The Minors,* Huntsville Stars, *Infinite Baseball Card Set,* Iowa Cubs, Jack Cain, Jack Donovan, *Jackson Sun,* Jacksonville Jumbo Shrimp, Jacksonville Suns, Jake Thompson, Jesse Goldberg-Strassler, Jim Garshow, Jim Tocco, John Nolan, John Thorn, Josh Jackson, Josh Suchon, *Journal and Tribune,* J.P. Shadrick, *Kansas City Times,* KARE, KBUR, Keith Bodie, KENS 5, *Kevin Saldana's Minor League Tidbits, KittyLeague.blogspot.com, Kitty League Chronology, KittyLeague.com,* KMSP, KPVI, Kraig Williams, Lake Elsinore Storm, Lake Erie Crushers, Lancaster JetHawks, Lansing Lugnuts, Las Vegas 51s, Las

Vegas Aviators, *Las Vegas Sun, Leagues of their Own: Independent Professional Baseball, 1993-2000,* Lehigh Valley IronPigs, *Library of Congress, Life in the Minors, Lights On! The Wild Century-Long Saga of Night Baseball,* Lizette Espinosa, *Log Cabin Democrat, Long Ball: The Legend and Lore of the Home Run, Los Angeles Evening Citizen News, Los Angeles Times, Louisville Courier-Journal,* Lowell Spinners, Mark Nasser, *Mason City Globe Gazette,* Matt Mika, Midwest League Guide, Mike Curto, Mike Richardson, *MiLB.com, Milwaukee Journal, Minneapolis Star, Minor League All-Star Teams, 1922-1962, MinorLeagueBaseball.com, Minor Miracles, Minor Moments, Major Memories,* Mississippi Braves, Missoula Osprey, Missoula PaddleHeads, *MLB.com, Modesto Bee,* Modesto Nuts, *Montana Baseball History, More Tales From the Dugout, Morning Journal,* Morrie Silver, *Muskogee Phoenix, Napa Valley Register, Nashville Public Radio,* Nashville Sounds, *National Association Guides,* National Baseball Hall of Fame Library, NationalPastime.com, NBC Bay Area, NBC Connecticut, NBC News, NESN, *Nevada State Journal, Never a Bad Game: 50 Years of the Southern League,* New England Historical Society, New Orleans Zephyrs, *News and Observer, News-Press, Newton Record, New York Clipper, New York Daily News, New York Times,* NJ.com, *No Minor Accomplishment: The Revival of New Jersey Professional Baseball, Oakland Tribune, Ogden Standard-Examiner,* Oklahoma City Dodgers, *Old Dominion Sun,* Omaha Storm Chasers, *On to Nicollet: The Glory and Fame of the Minneapolis Millers, Oshkosh Northwestern, Ottawa Citizen, Our Sports Central, Outlaw Ballplayers: Interviews and Profiles from the Independent Carolina League, Out of the Park – Memoir of a Minor League All-Star, Outsider Baseball, Pacific Coast League Date Book, Pacific Coast League Sketch & Record Book, Palm Beach Post, Pasadena Post,* Paul Braverman, Pawtucket Red Sox, Pensacola Blue Wahoos, *Pittsburgh Daily Post,* Portland Beavers, *Post and Courier, Post-Register,* Potomac Nationals, *Press and Sun-Bulletin, Press-Enterprise,* Quizlet History of Baseball Flash Cards, Rancho Cucamonga Quakes, Randy Bush, Randy Wehofer, *Rapid City Journal, Reach Base Ball Guides, Reach's Official American League Base Ball Guide, Record-Argus,* Reno Aces, *Reno Gazette-Journal, Retrosheet.org,* Rich Burk, Richmond Flying Squirrels, *Rickwood*

Field, *Rochester Democrat and Chronicle,* Rochester Red Wings, *Rock Island Argus,* Rocky Mountain Vibes, *Rocky Mount Telegram, Root for the Home Team: Minor League Baseball's Most Off-the-Wall Team Names and the Stories Behind Them,* Roswell Daily Record, *Runs, Hits, and an Era: The Pacific Coast League, 1903-1958,* Russ Langer, SABR BioProject, *Sacramento Bee,* Sacramento River Cats, *Safe by a Mile, Salt Lake Tribune, St. Cloud Times, St. Louis Globe-Democrat, St. Louis Post-Dispatch, St. Paul Pioneer Press,* St. Paul Saints, Sam Dykstra, *San Antonio at Bat: Professional Baseball in the Alamo City, San Antonio Express-News, San Diego Union-Tribune, San Francisco Examiner, San Francisco Morning Call,* San Rafael Pacifics, *Santa Cruz Sentinel, Santa Fe New Mexican,* Savannah Sand Gnats, *SB Nation,* Scott Sailor, S. Derby Gisclair, *Sea Coast Echo, Seattle Times, Separating the Men From the Boys: The First Half Century of the Carolina League, Shawnee Sun, Shreveport Journal, Shreveport Times,* Society for American Baseball Research, *Some of My Best Friends are Crazy, South Bend Tribune,* Southern League, *Spalding Baseball Guides, Spalding's Official Base Ball Records, Spokane Daily Chronicle, Spokesman-Review, Sporting Life, Sporting News, Sporting News Official Baseball Guides, Sports Illustrated,* SportsNet New York, *Sports Press Northwest, Star Tribune, Stateline Legends of Sports, Staten Island Advance, Staying Out Late Under a Full Moon,* Steve DeSalvo, Steven Ericson, Steve Hyder, Steve Keyman, Steve Klauke, Steve Selby, Steve Wendt, *Stolen Season, Storied Stadiums, Syracuse.com,* Tacoma Rainiers, *Tales From the Ballpark, Tallahassee Democrat, Tampa Bay Times,* Tennessee Smokies, Terry Kennedy, *Texas League Baseball, 1888-1958, Texas League Baseball Almanac, The 26th Man, The Athletic, The Bee, The Bilko Athletic Club, The Californian, The Catcher was a Lady, The Chattanooga Lookouts & 100 Seasons of Scenic City Baseball, The Courier, The Diamonds of Dixie: Travels Through the Southern Minor Leagues, The Encyclopedia of Minor League Baseball, The Gazette, The Greatest Minor League: A History of the Pacific Coast League, 1903-1957, The Hardball Times, The Journal, The KOM League Remembered, The Middle Atlantic League 1922-1952, The Minor Leagues, The Minors, The National Game, Second Edition, The New England League: A Baseball History 1885-1949,*

The Not-So Minor Leagues, The Oklahoman, The Oregonian, The Rise of Milwaukee Baseball, The Rocks: The True Story of the Worst Team in Baseball History, The Southern League, The Story of Minor League Baseball, The Sun News, The Tennessean, The Texas League 1888-1987: A Century of Baseball, The Twenty-Four Inch Home Run, The Vindicator Printing Company, *The Western League – A Baseball History, Three-Eye.com,* Tim Dillard, *Times News, Times-Picayune, Times Recorder, Times-Tribune,* Tim Grubbs, Todd Musburger, Tom Kotchman, Tommy Lasorda, Tom Nichols, Tony Muser, Toronto Blue Jays, Tri-City ValleyCats, *Twilight of the Long-Ball Gods,* Twins Daily, *Ty Cobb: A Terrible Beauty,* Tyler Maun, *United Press International, USA Today, Valley Morning Star, Vicksburg Evening Post,* Visalia Rawhide, *Wall Street Journal, Washington Post, Waterloo-Cedar Falls Courier,* WBOC-TV, West Virginia Public Broadcasting, *We Would Have Played Forever: The Story of the Coastal Plain Baseball League, Wheeling Daily Register,* WHP-TV, *Wichita Beacon, Wild and Outside: How a Renegade Minor League Revived the Spirit of Baseball in America's Heartland, Williamsport Sun-Gazette,* Wilmington Blue Rocks, *Wilmington Star News, Winnipeg Free Press,* Winnipeg Goldeyes, *Winston-Salem Journal,* WRAL, WTOP, WTSP 10 News, Wynn Montgomery, Wyoming State Museum, *Yahoo! Sports,* Zack Bayrouty.

ABOUT CIDER MILL PRESS
BOOK PUBLISHERS

Good ideas ripen with time. From seed to harvest, Cider Mill Press brings fine reading, information, and entertainment together between the covers of its creatively crafted books. Our Cider Mill bears fruit twice a year, publishing a new crop of titles each spring and fall.

"Where good books are ready for press"
501 Nelson Place
Nashville, Tennessee 37214

cidermillpress.com